Coloring Dragons
Volume 2

by
Nina Bolen

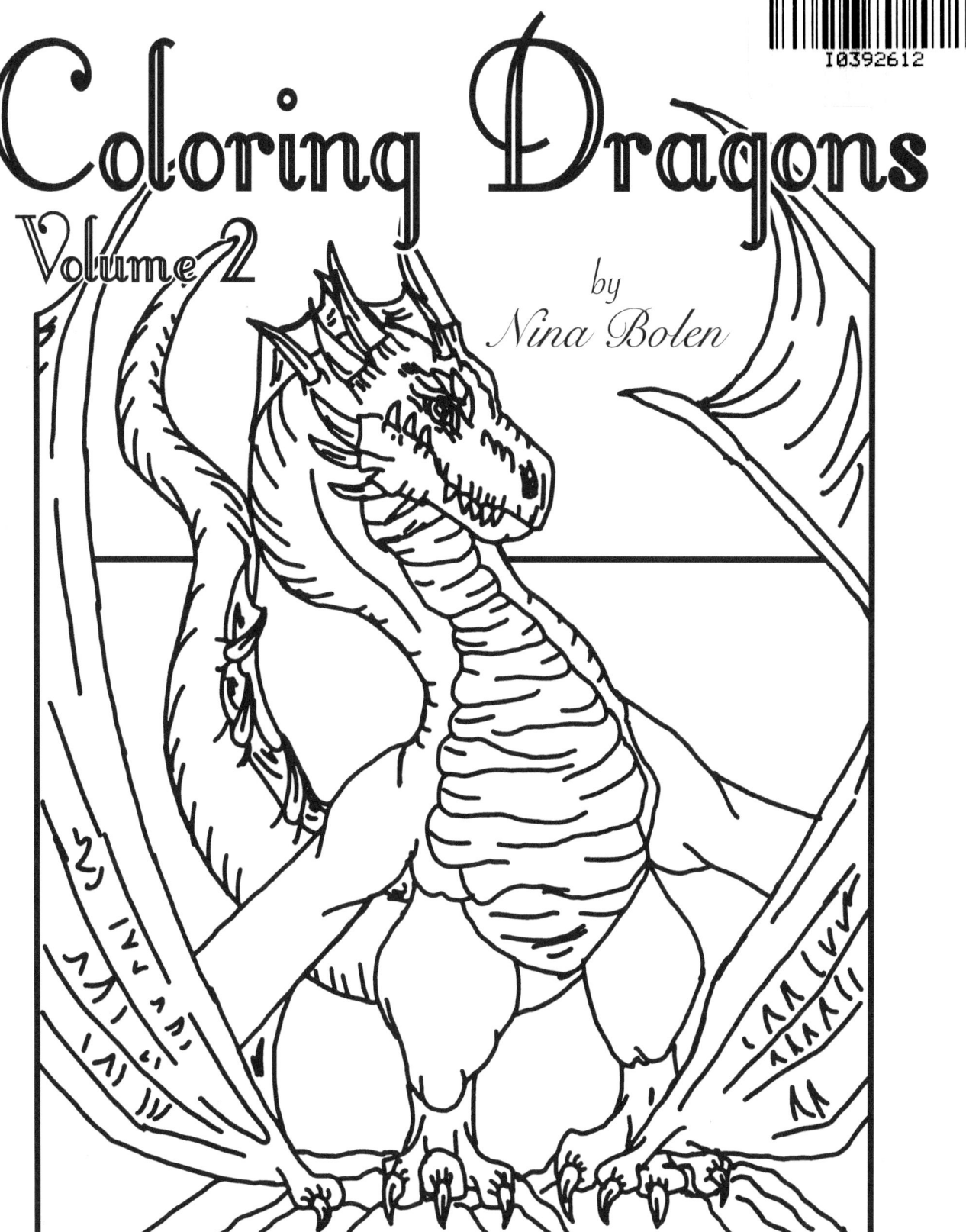

Artwork by Nina Bolen

Layout and Design by Brian Bolen

Find more artwork by Nina Bolen by visiting online at http://www.ninabolenart.com
Follow Nina on Facebook at https://www.facebook.com/NinaBolenArt

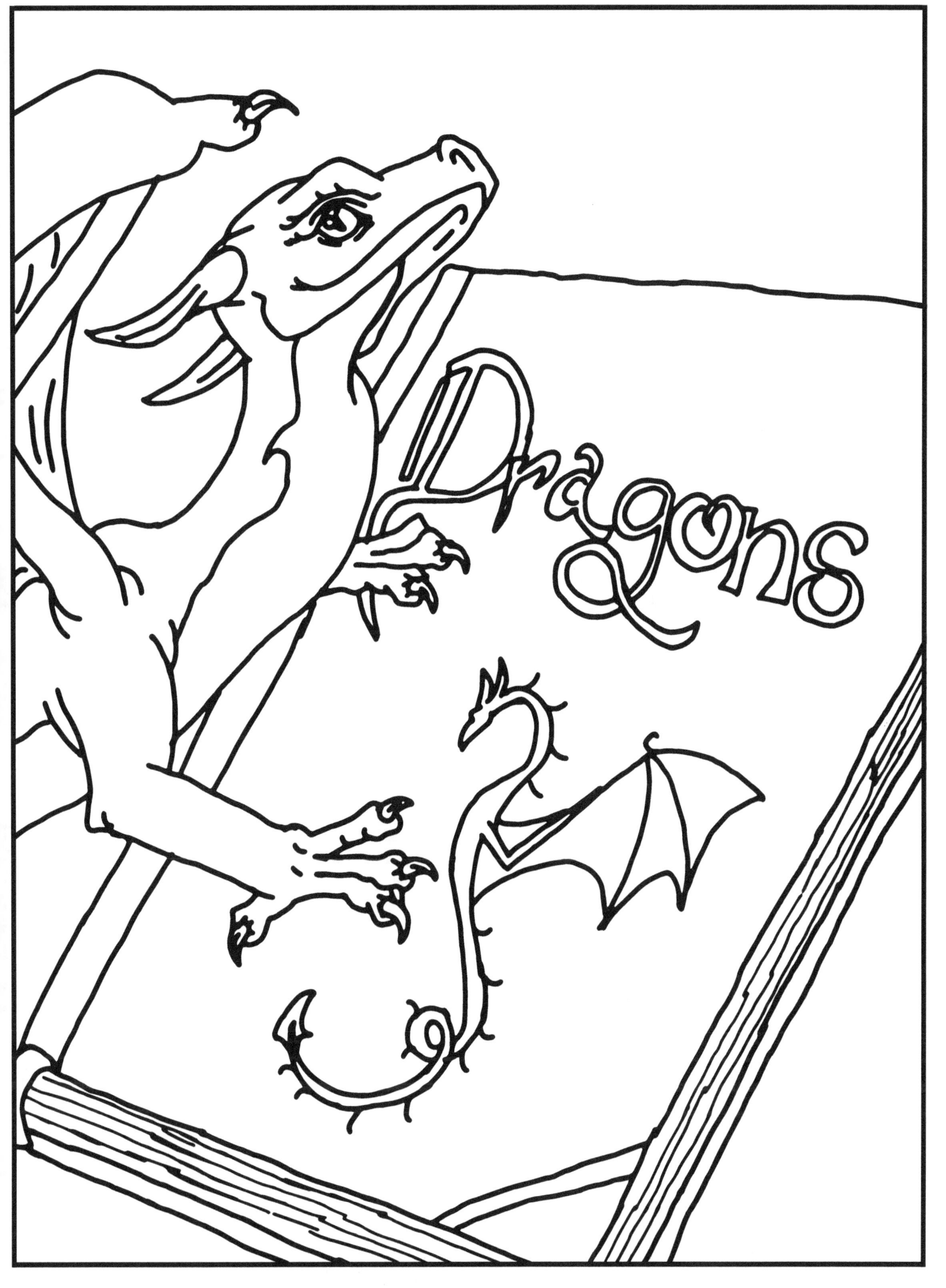

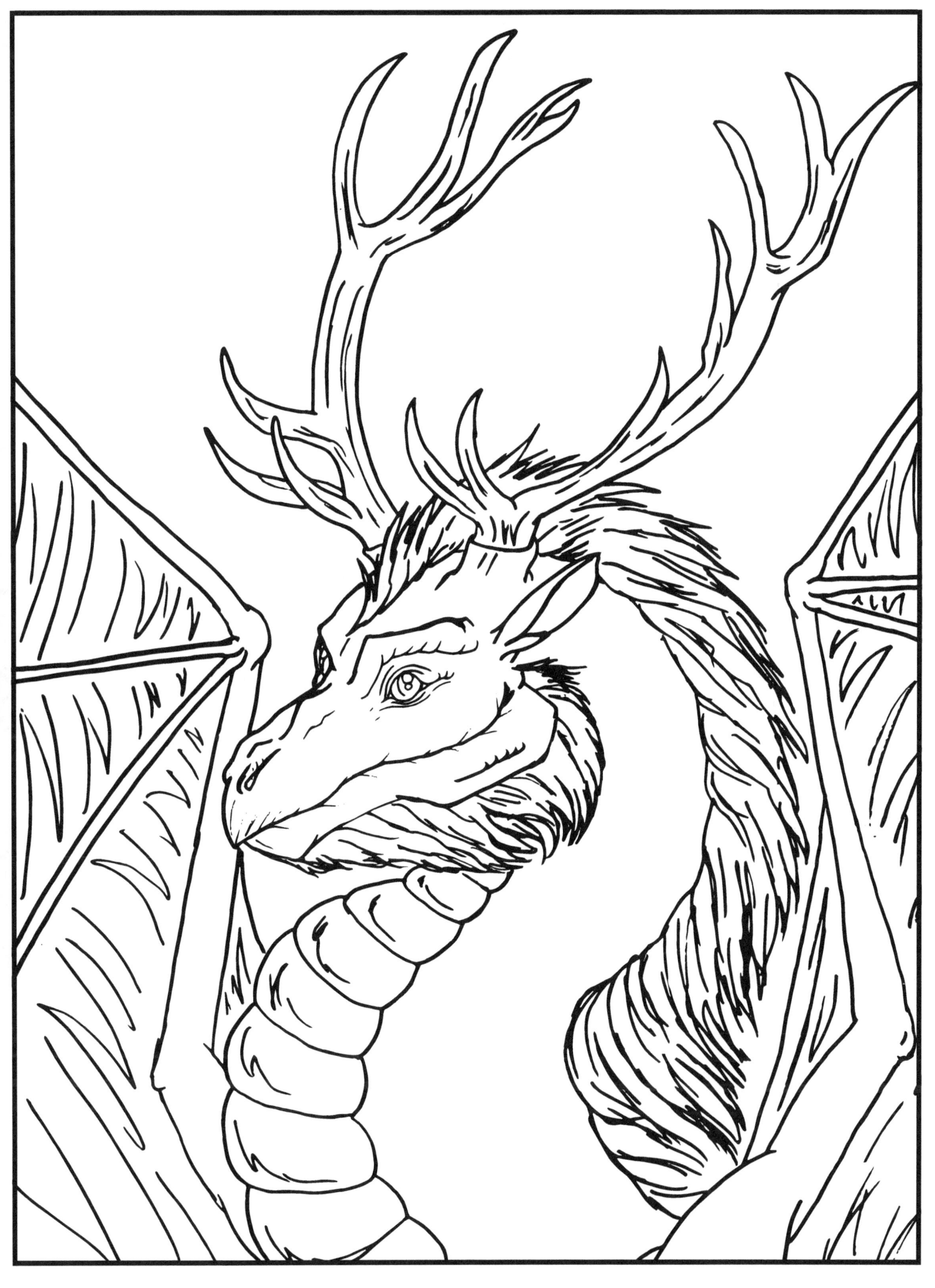

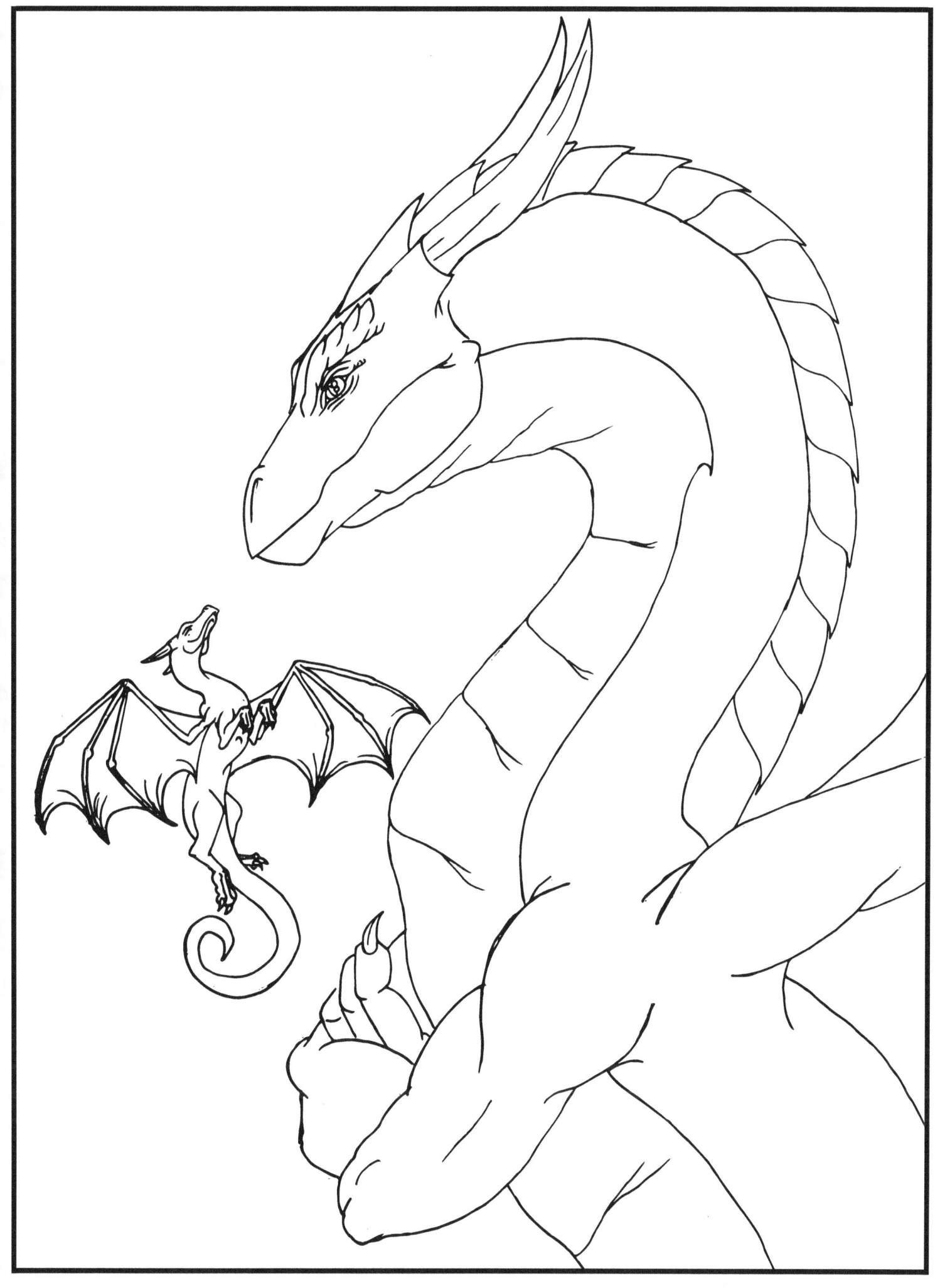

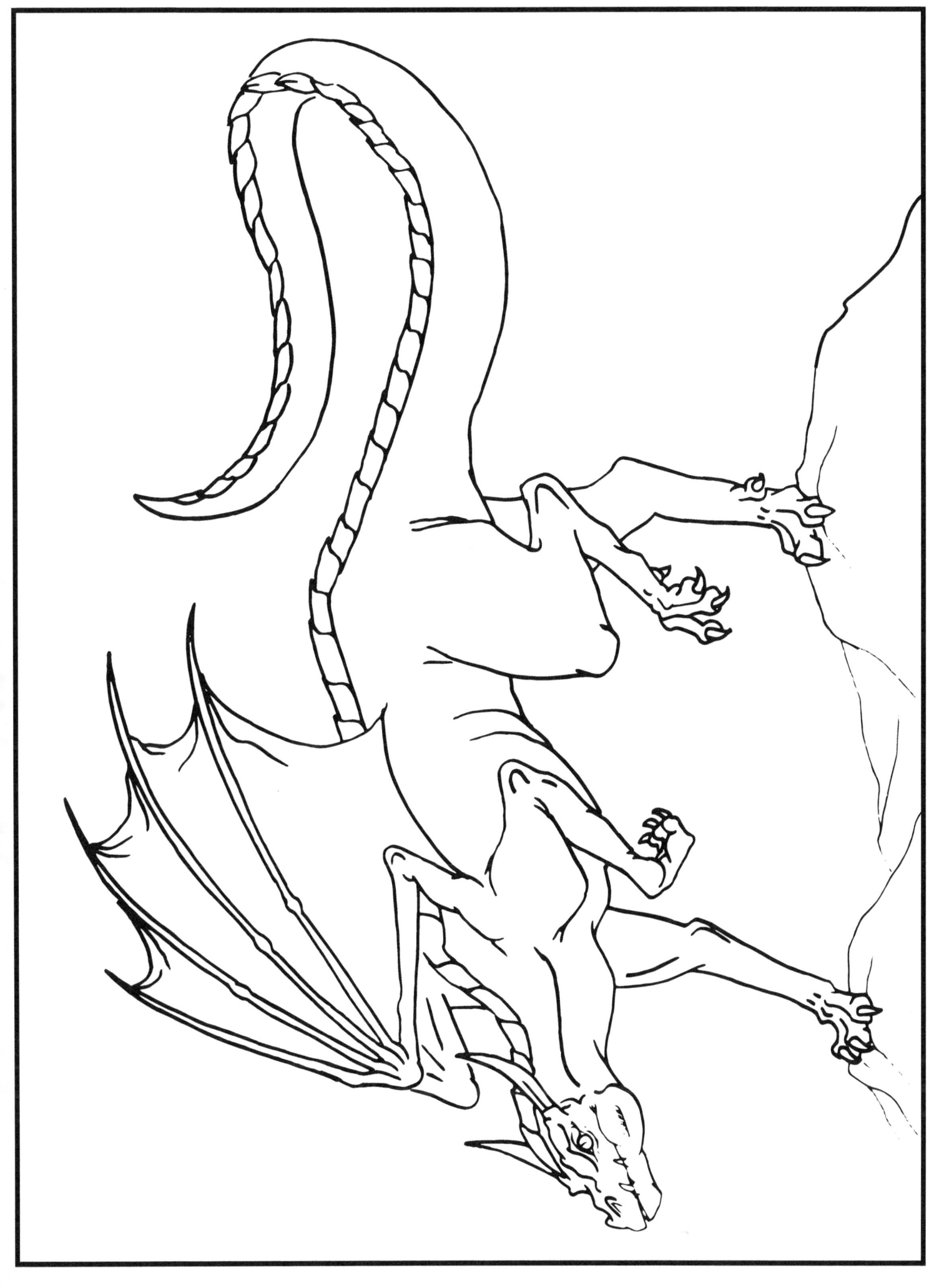

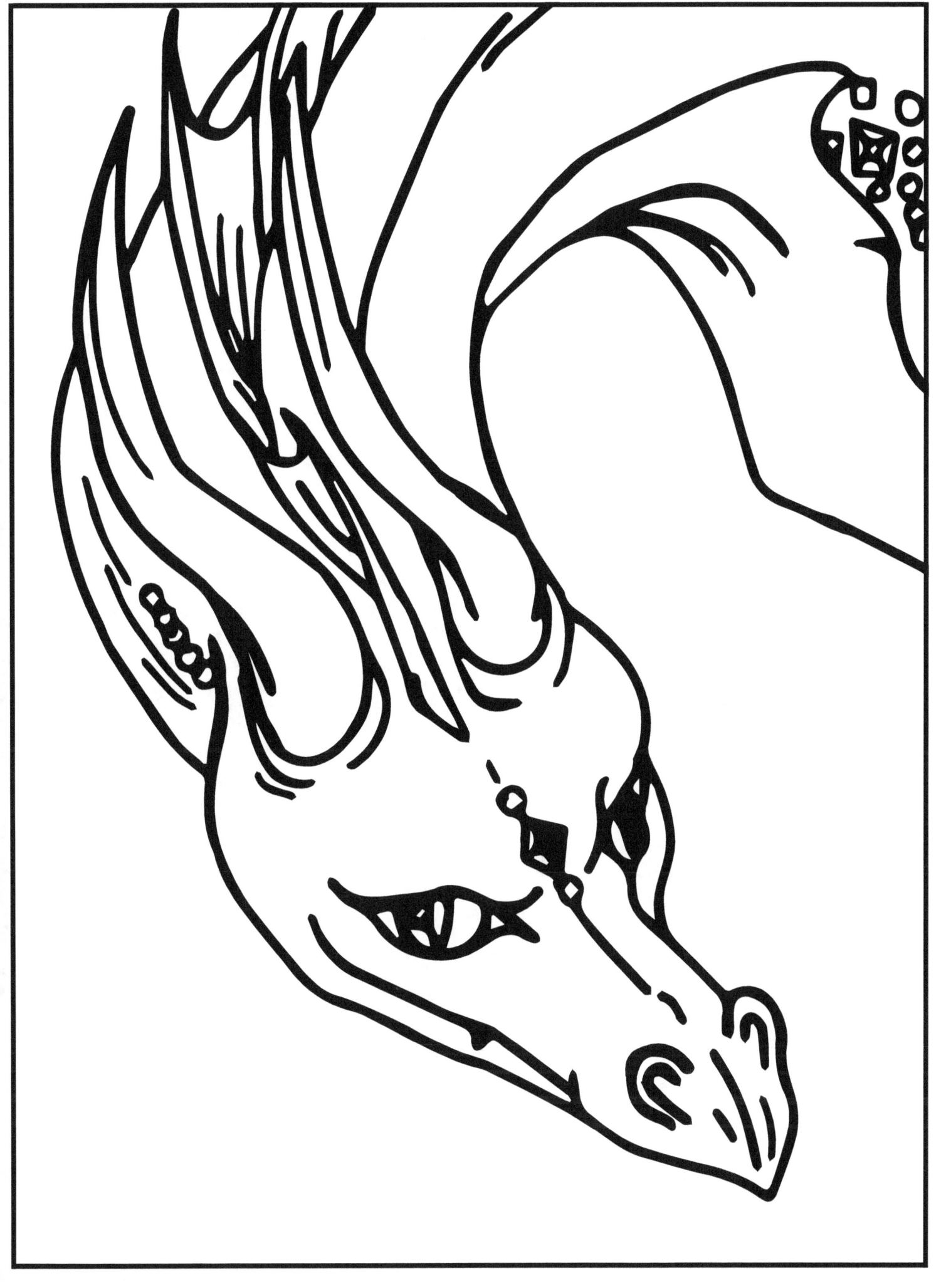

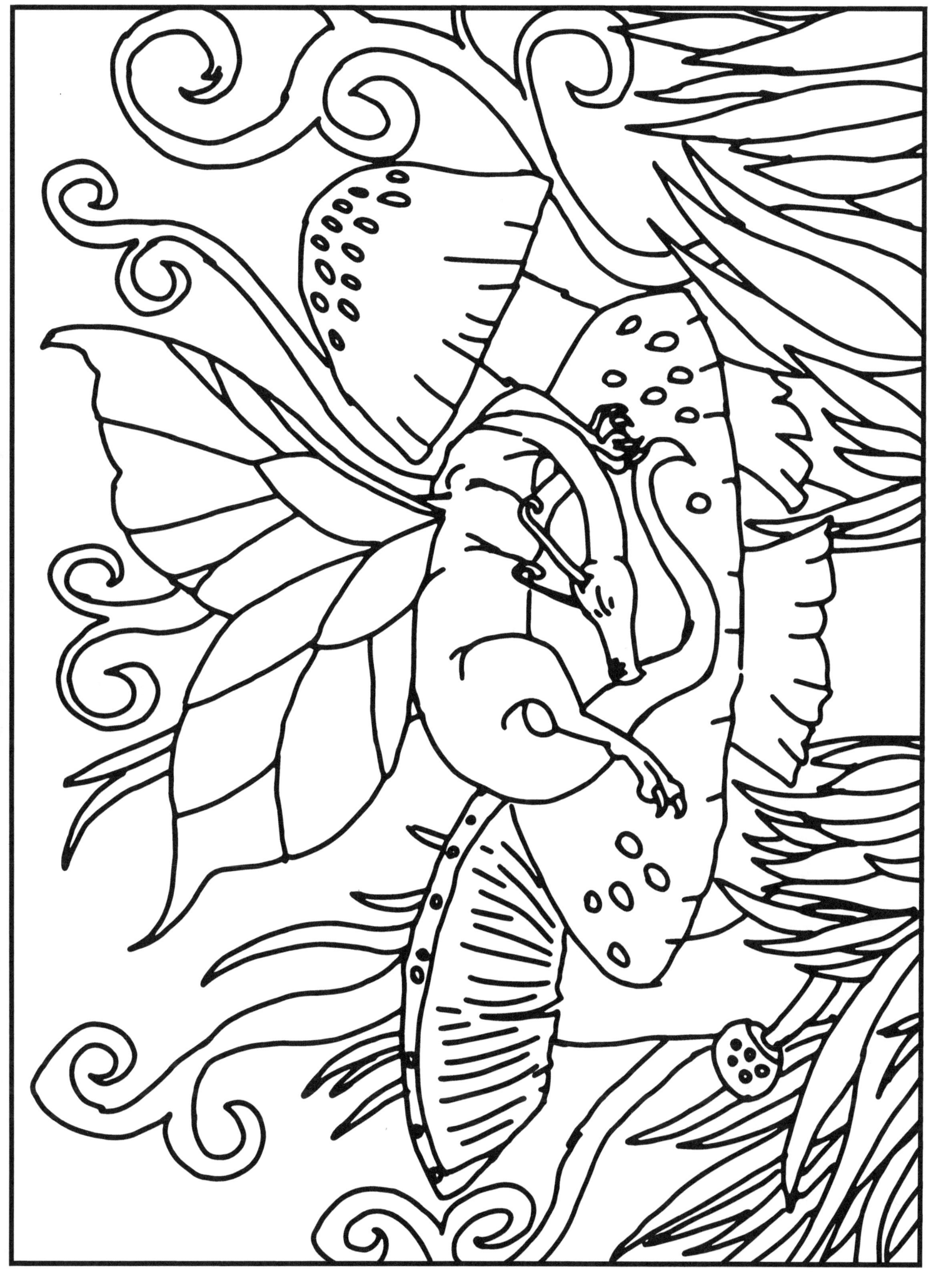

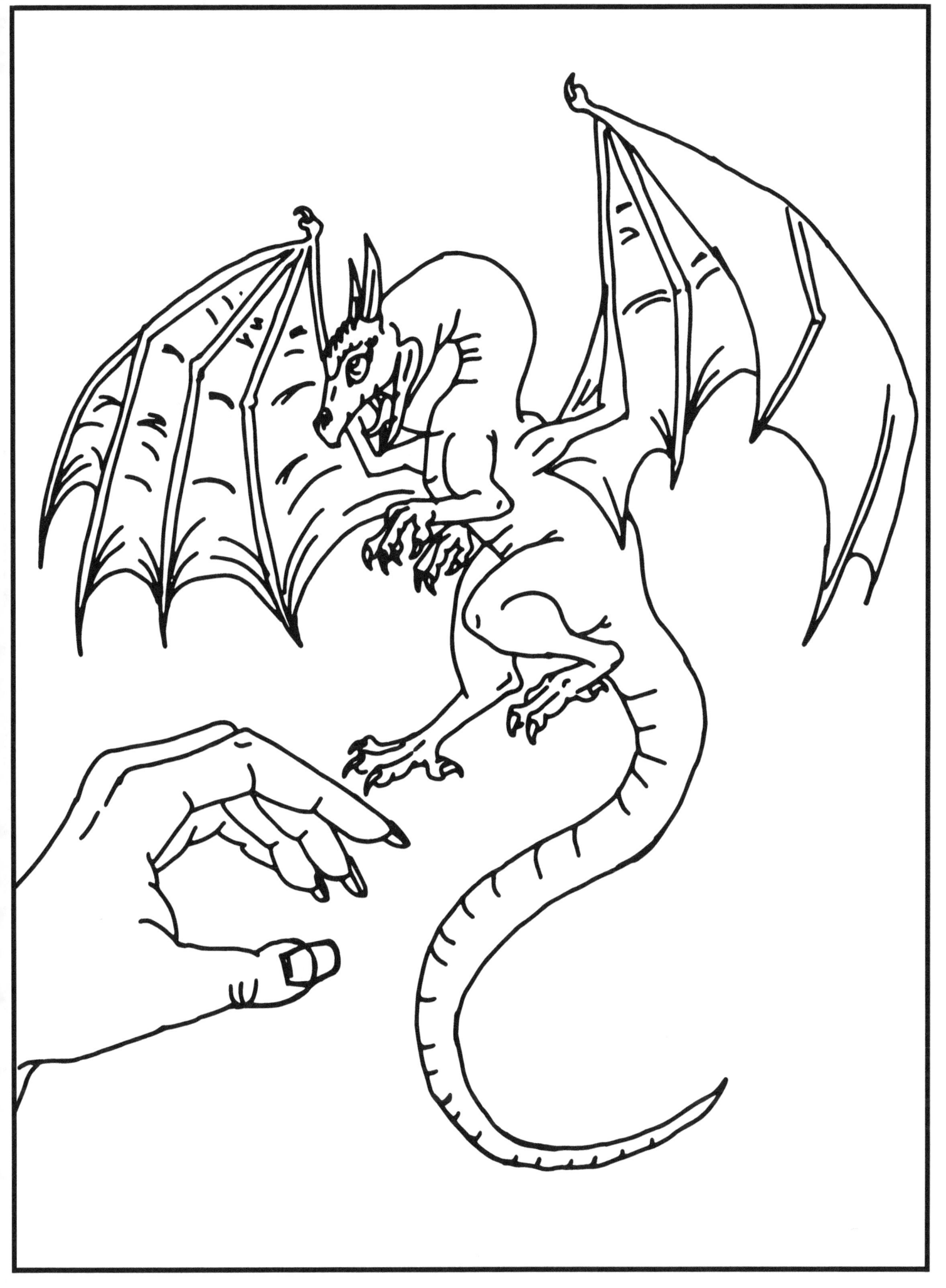

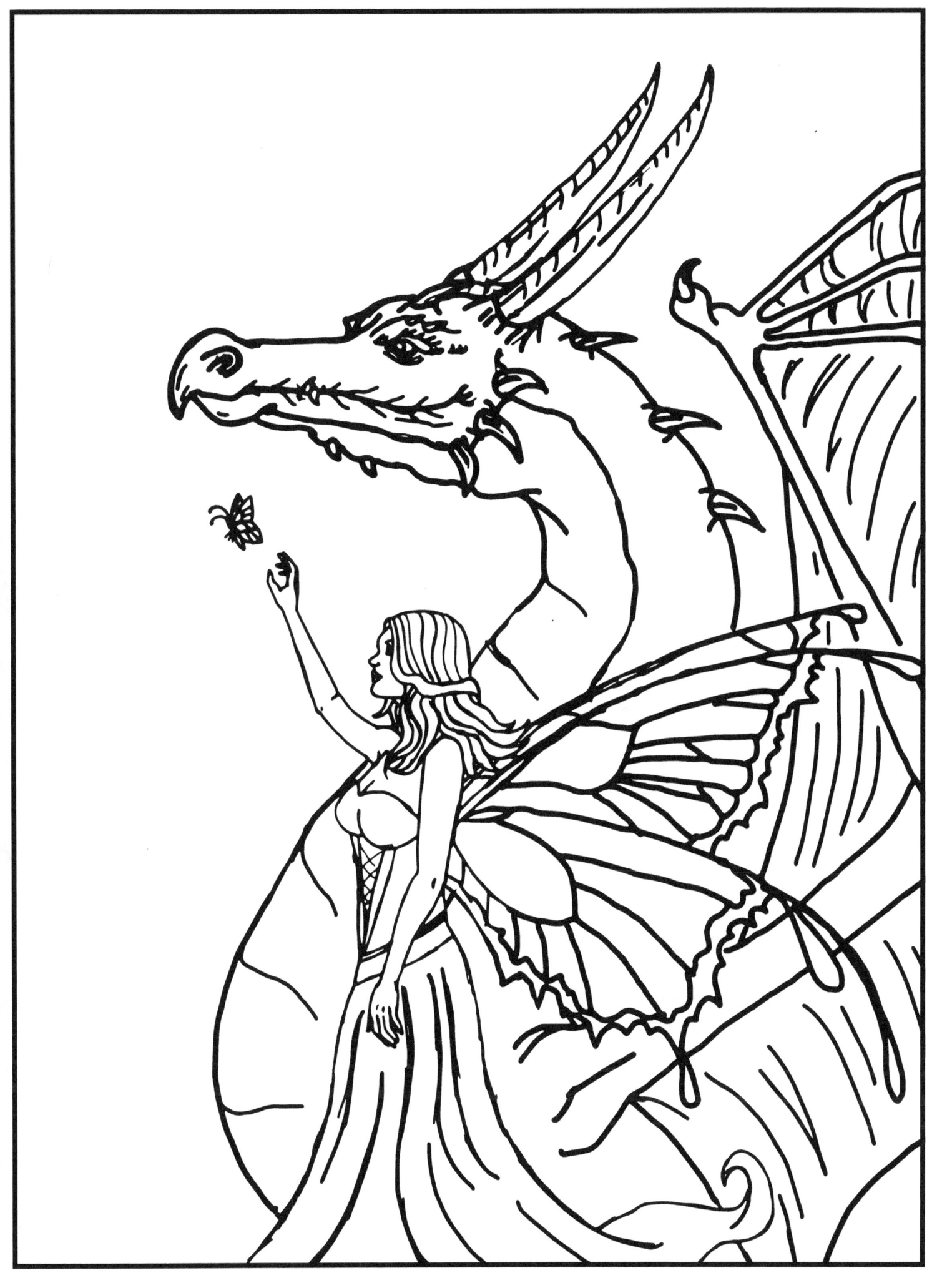

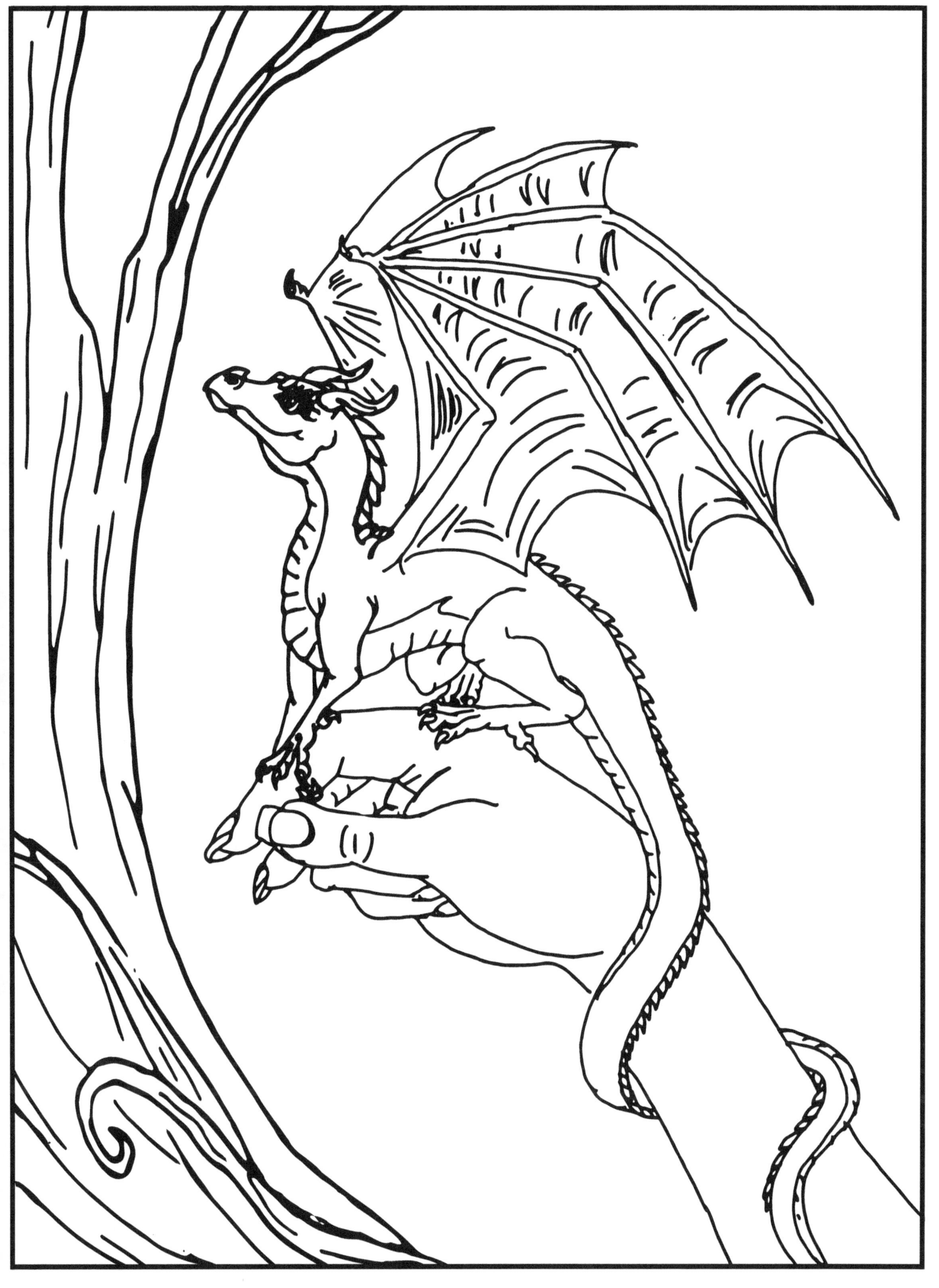

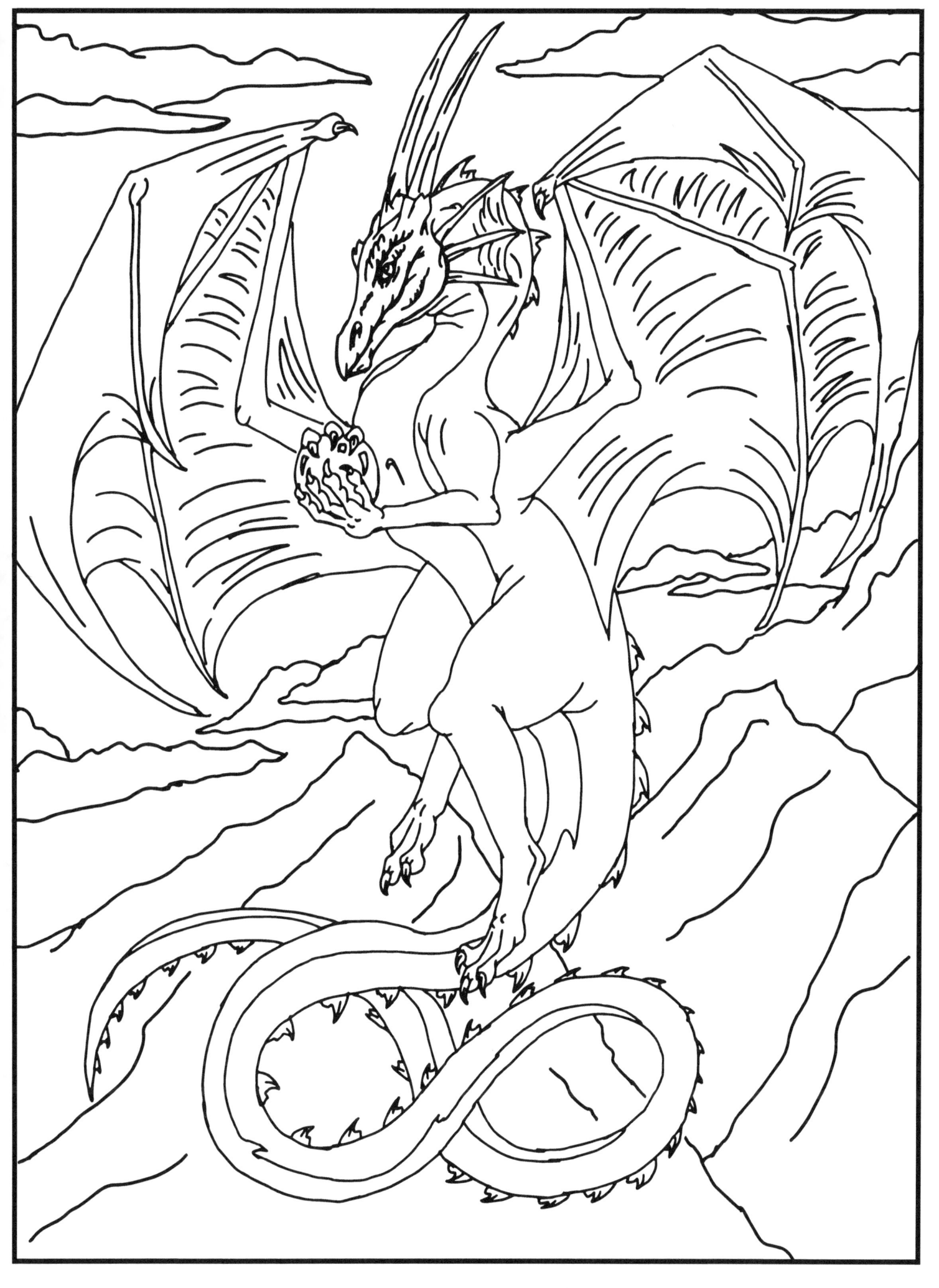

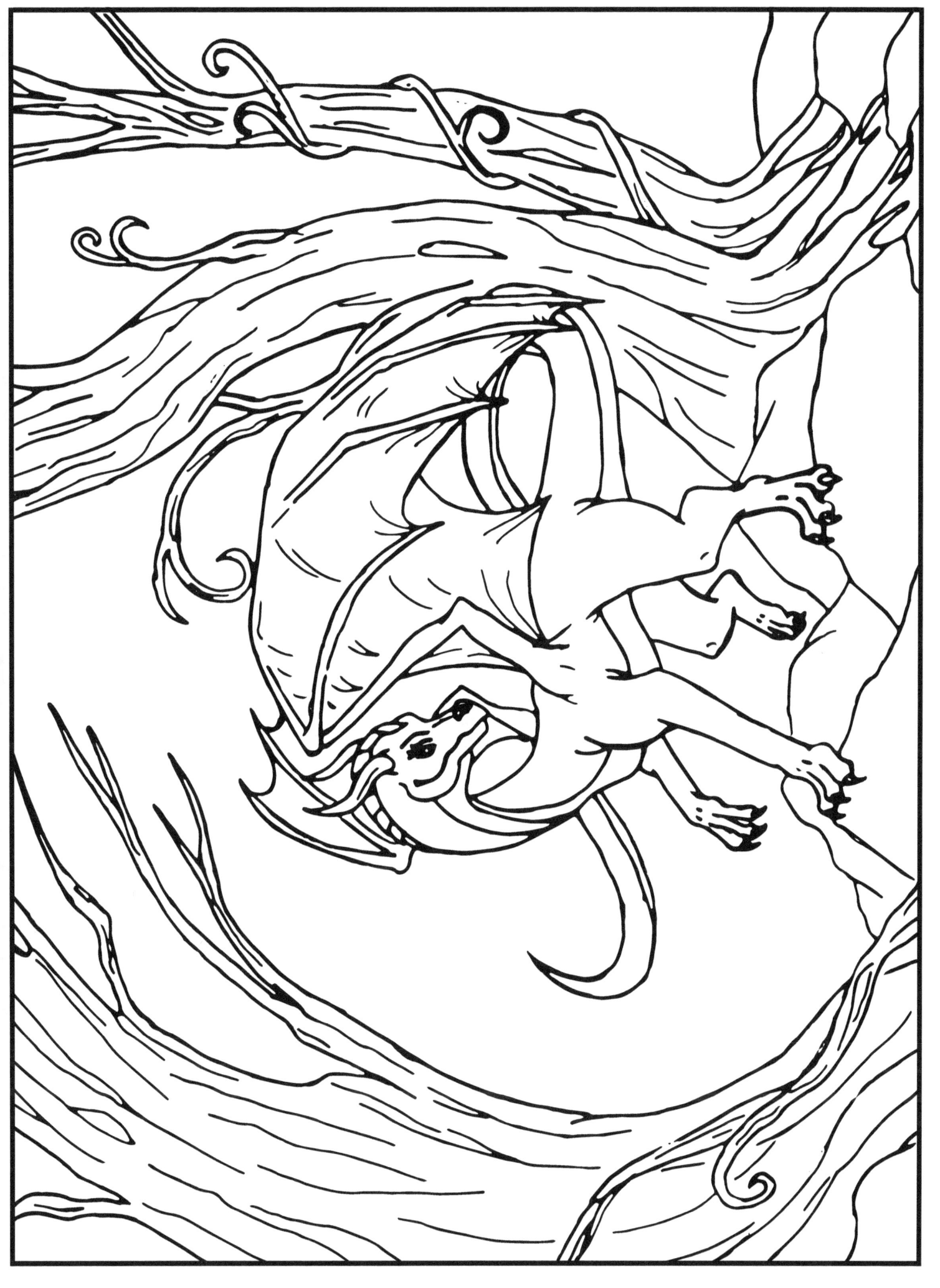

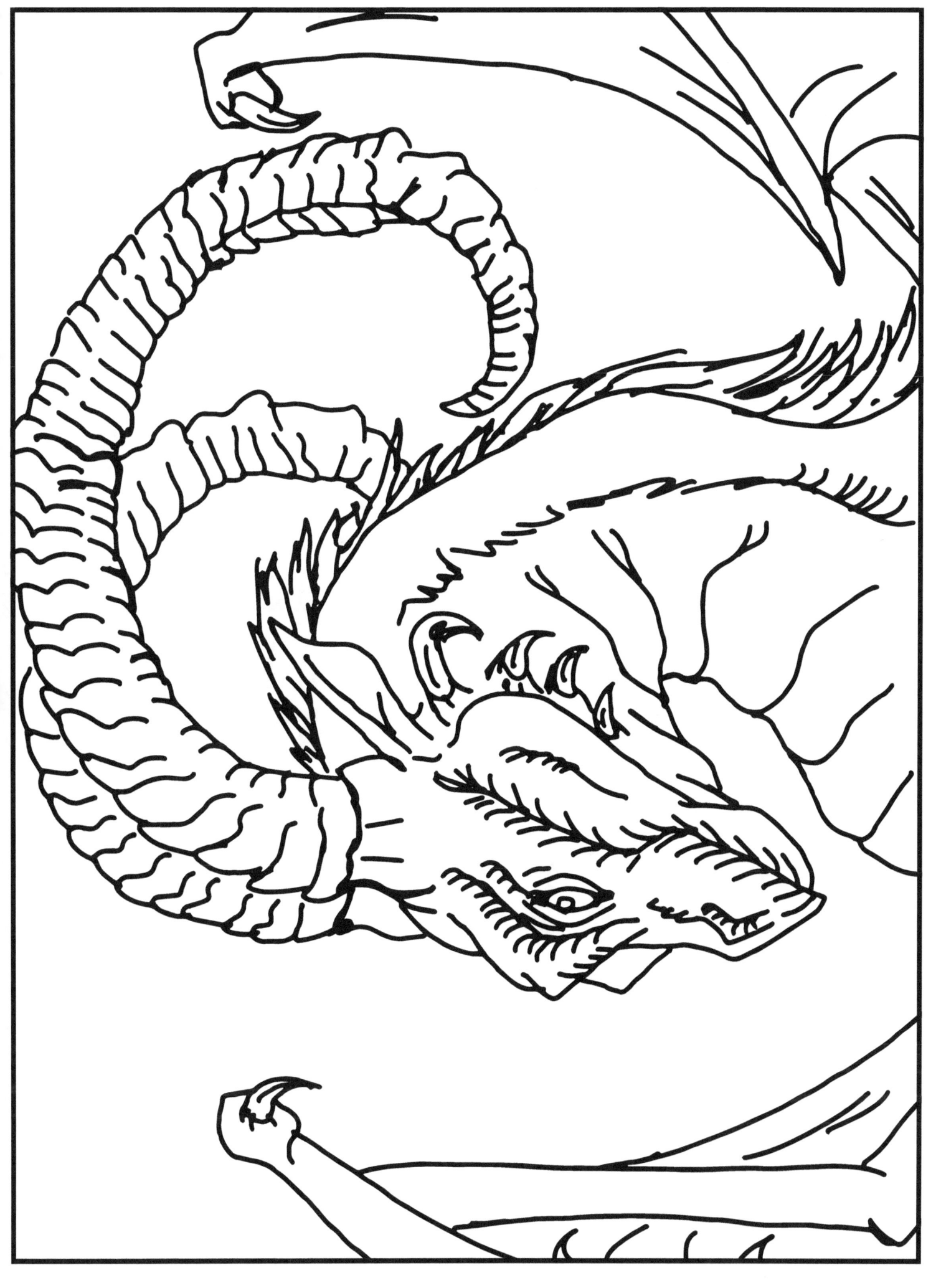

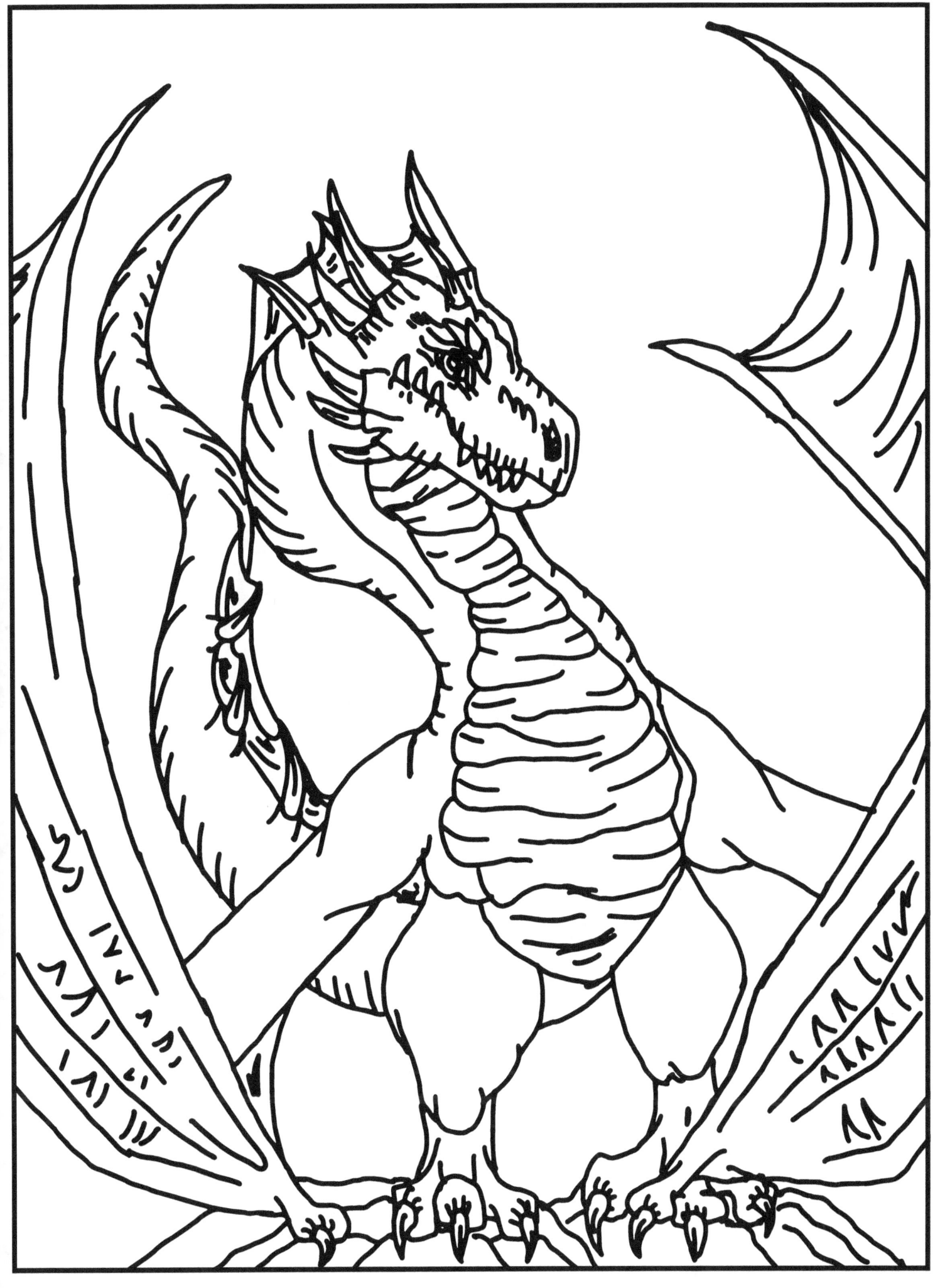

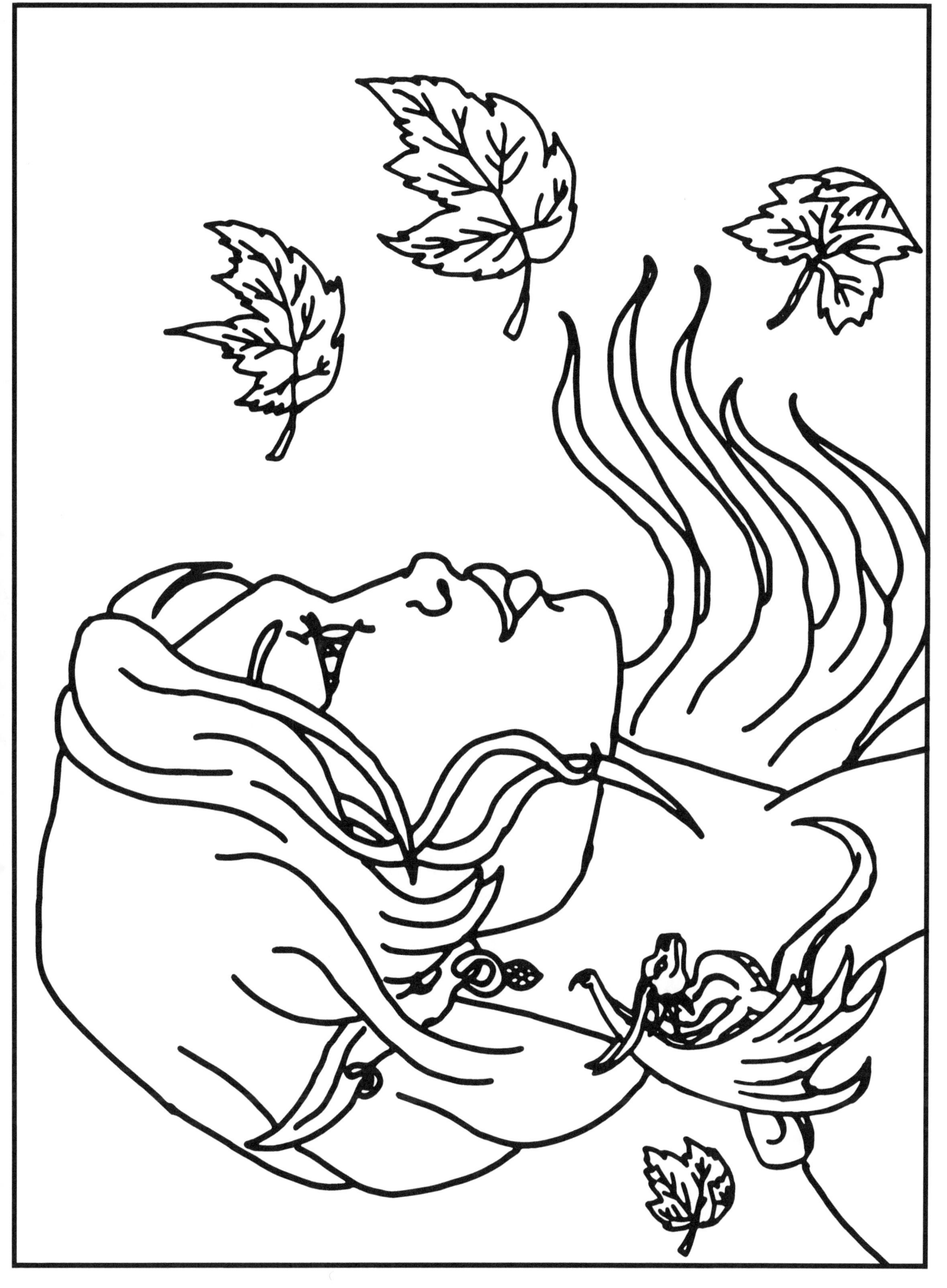

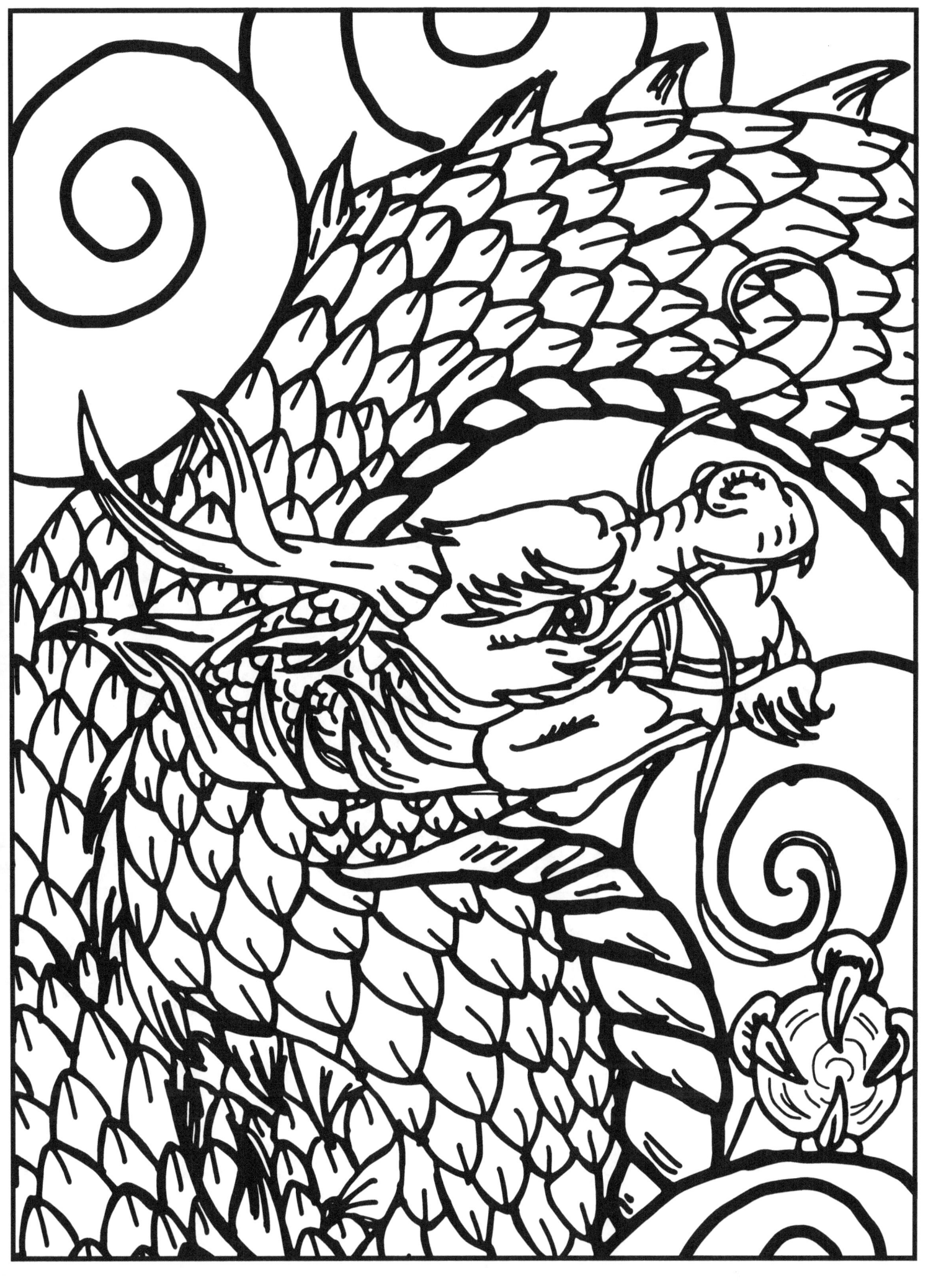

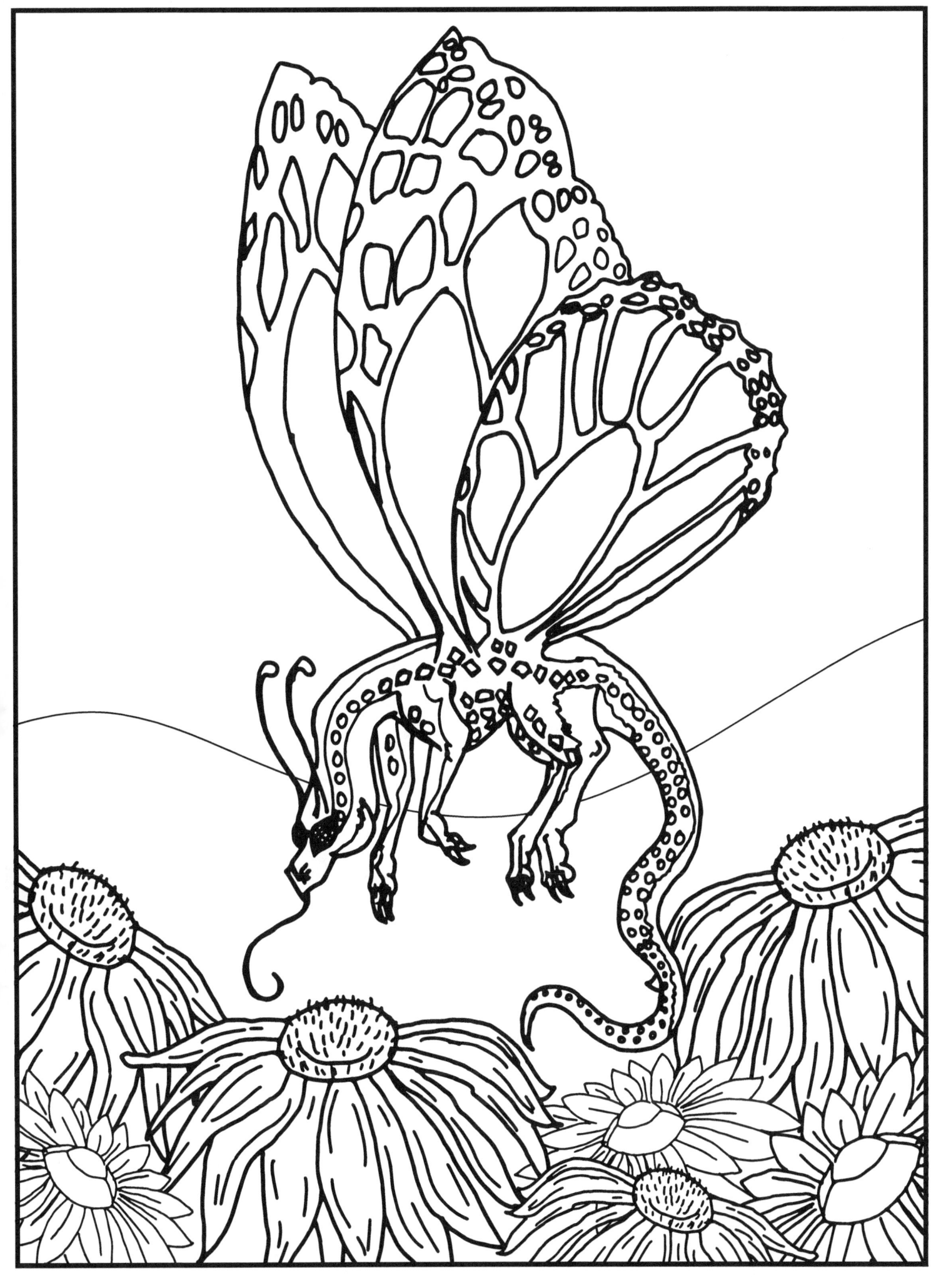

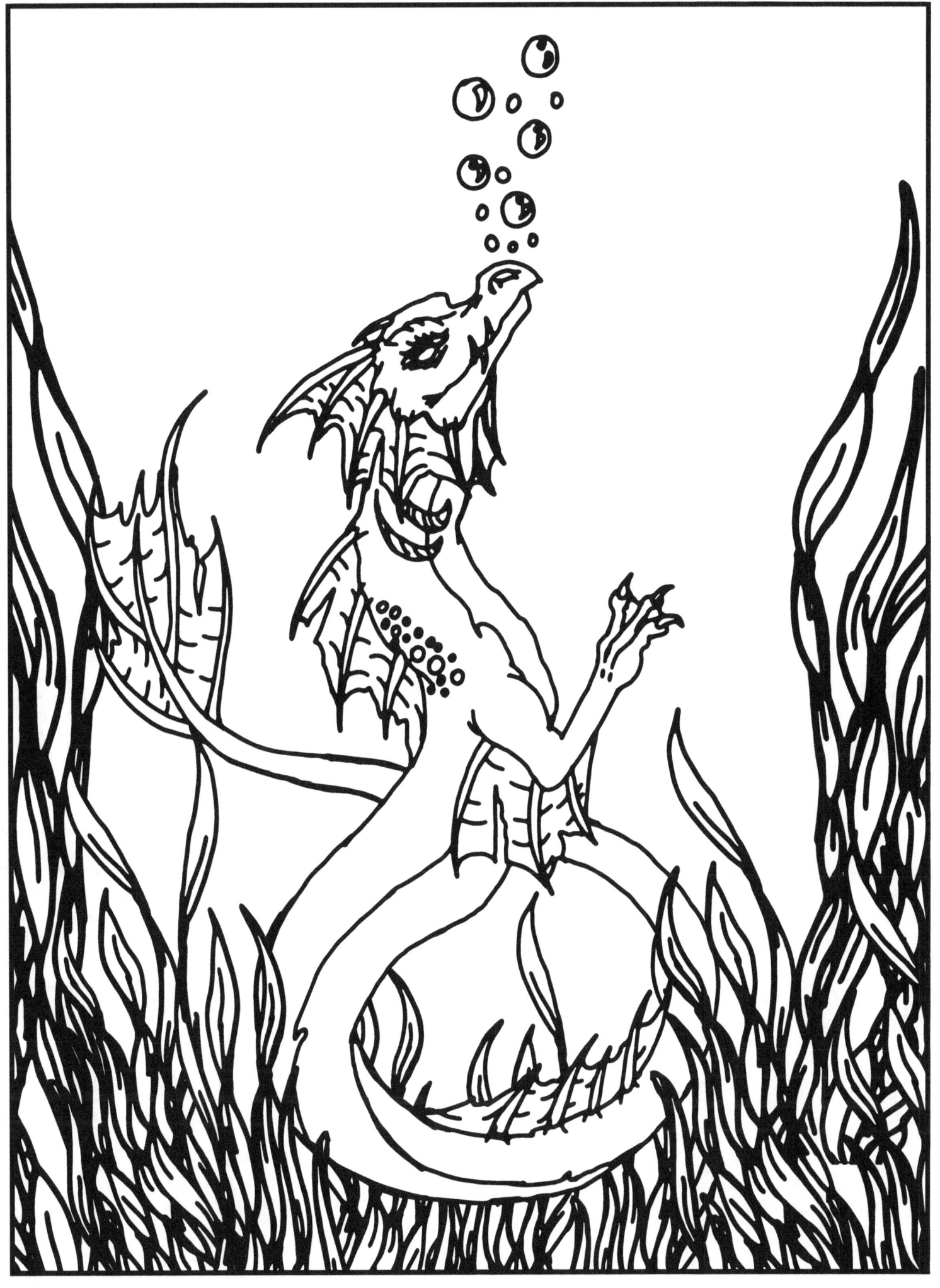

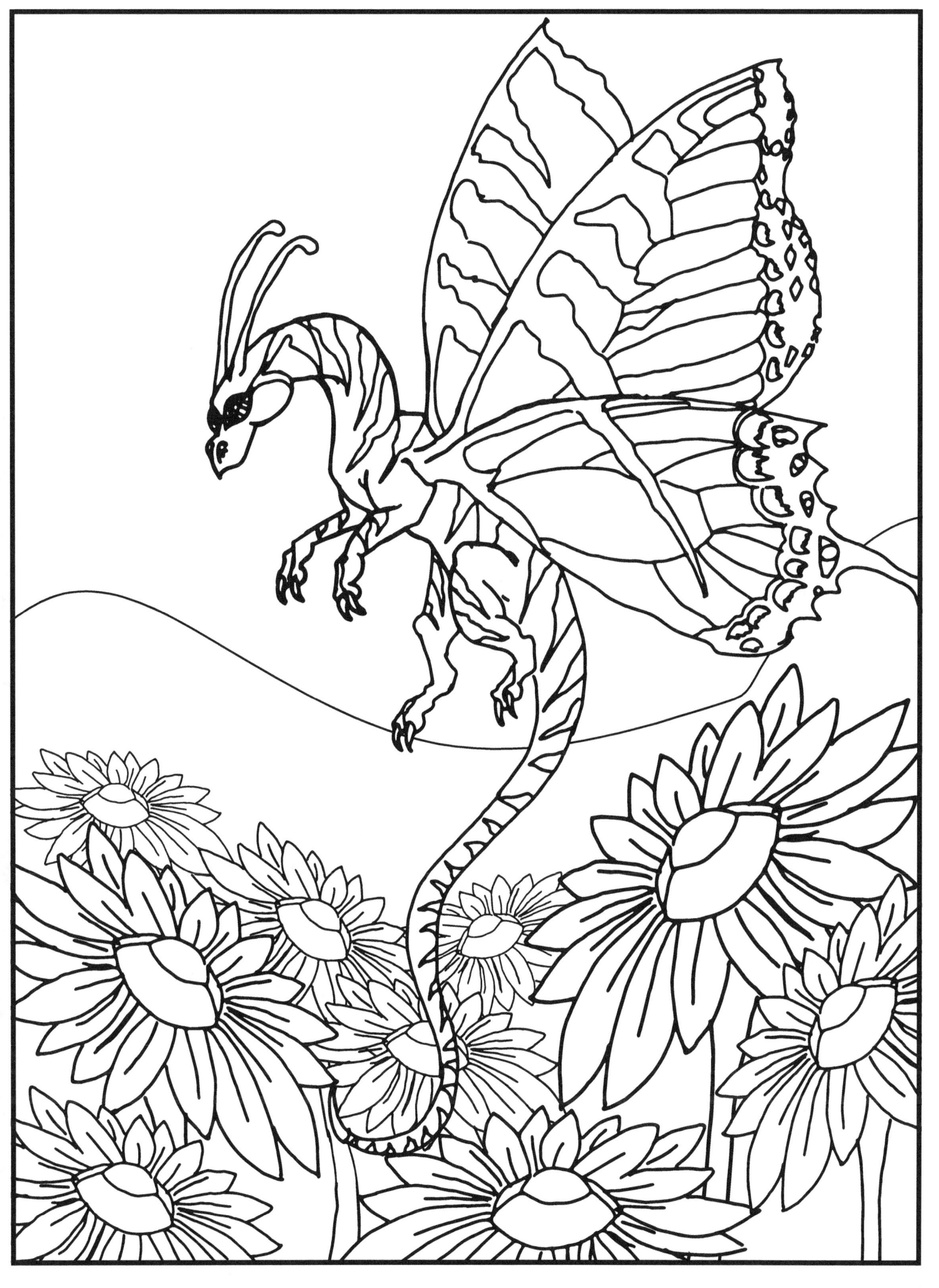

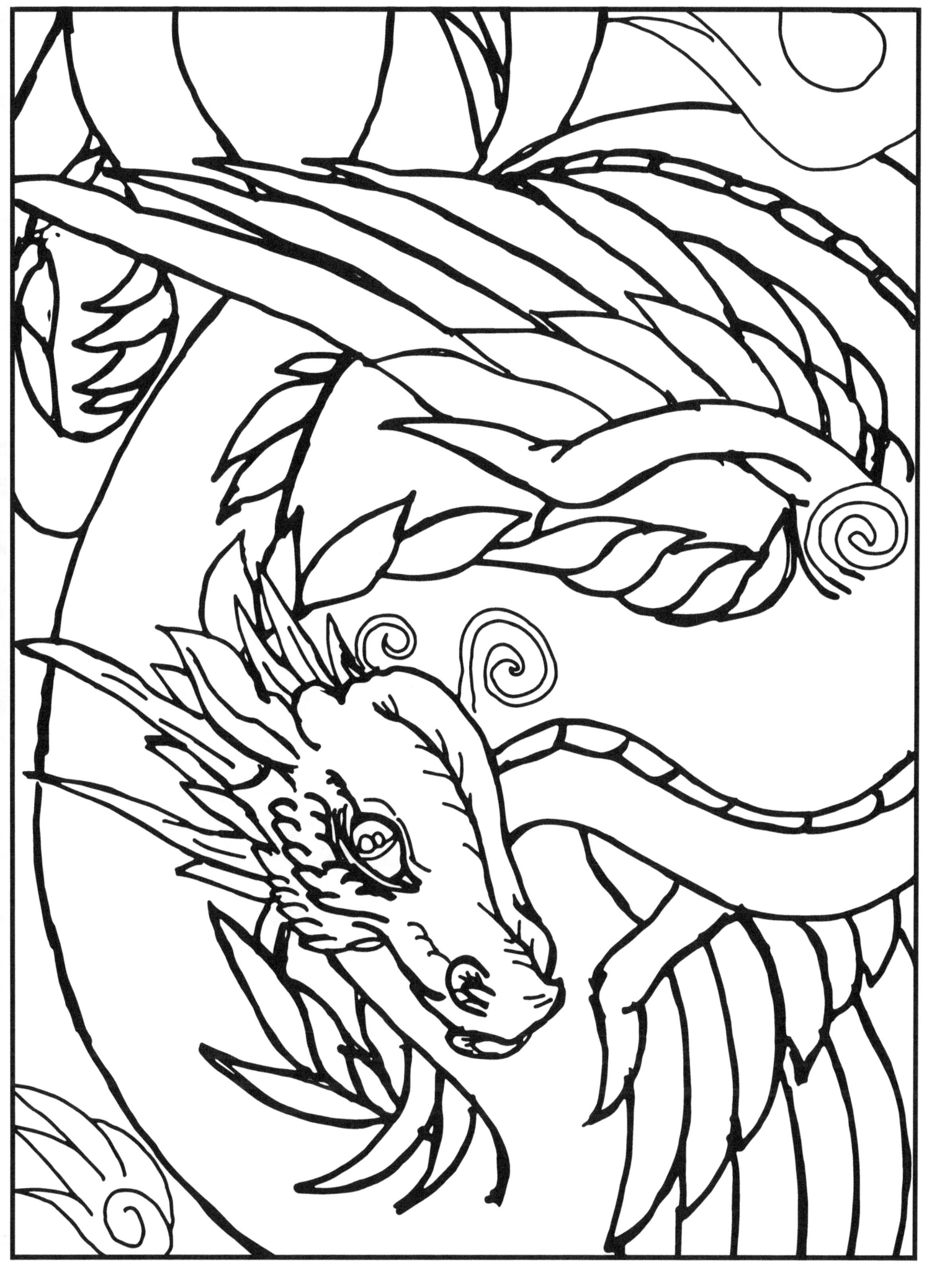

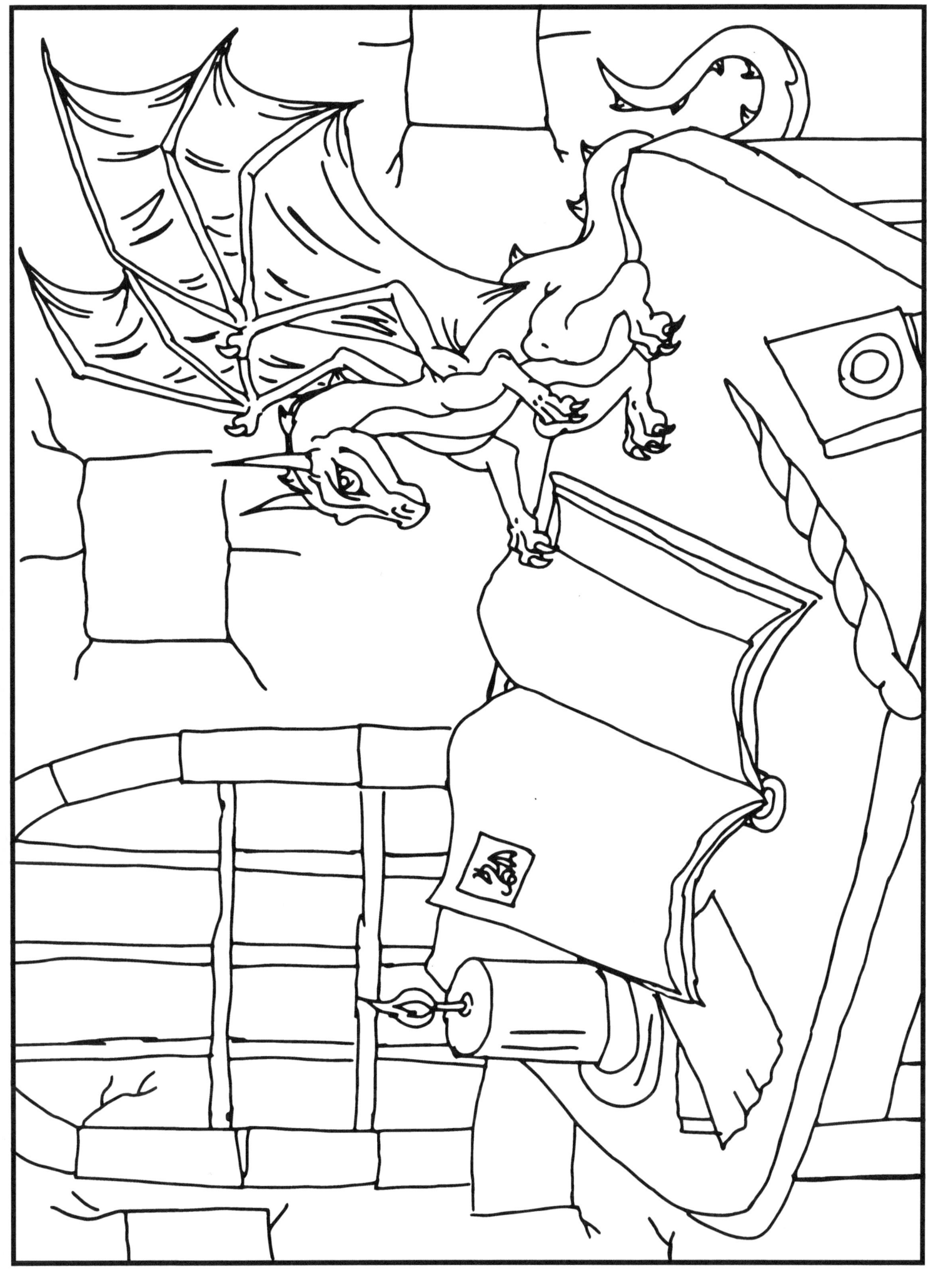

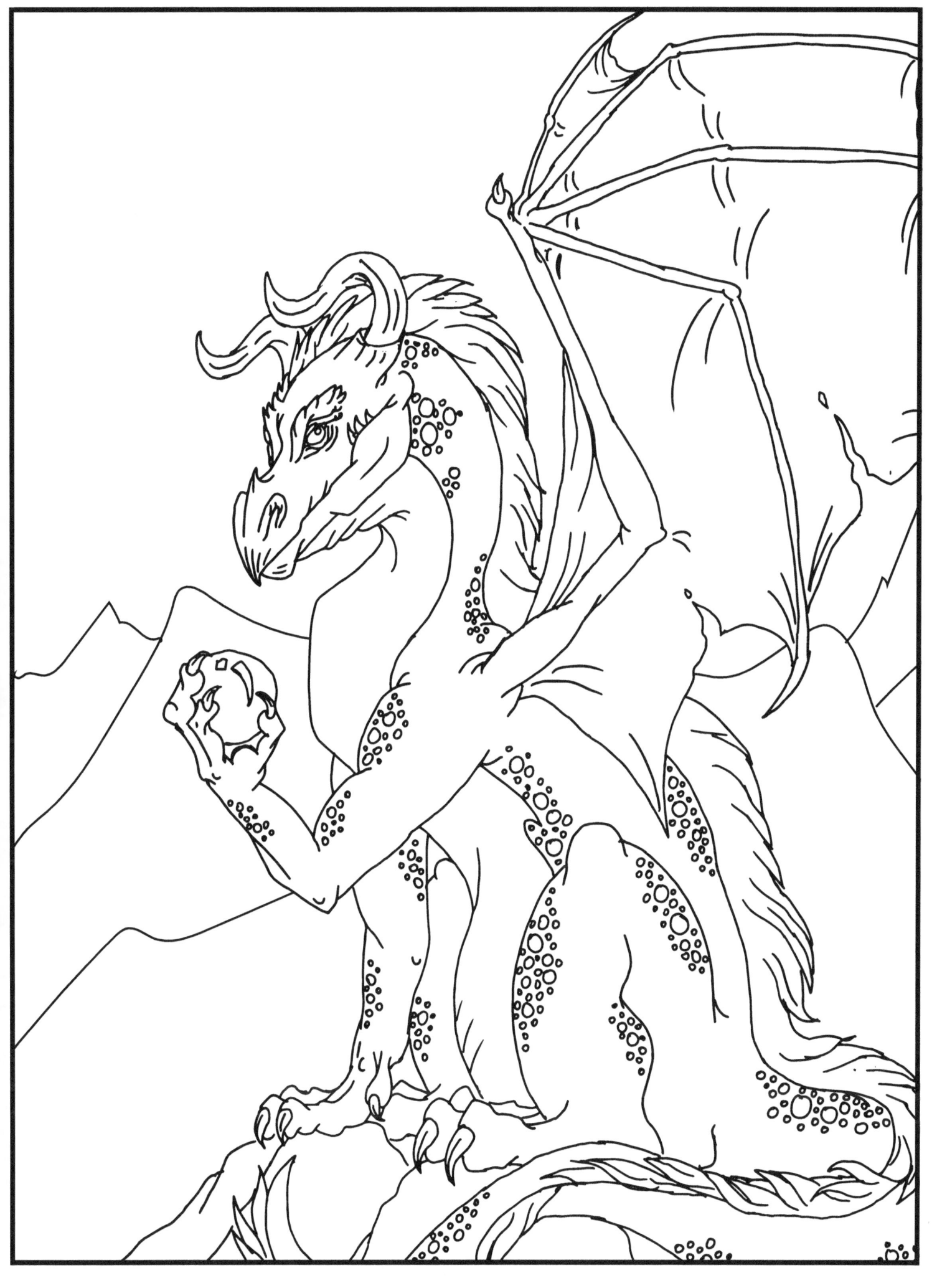

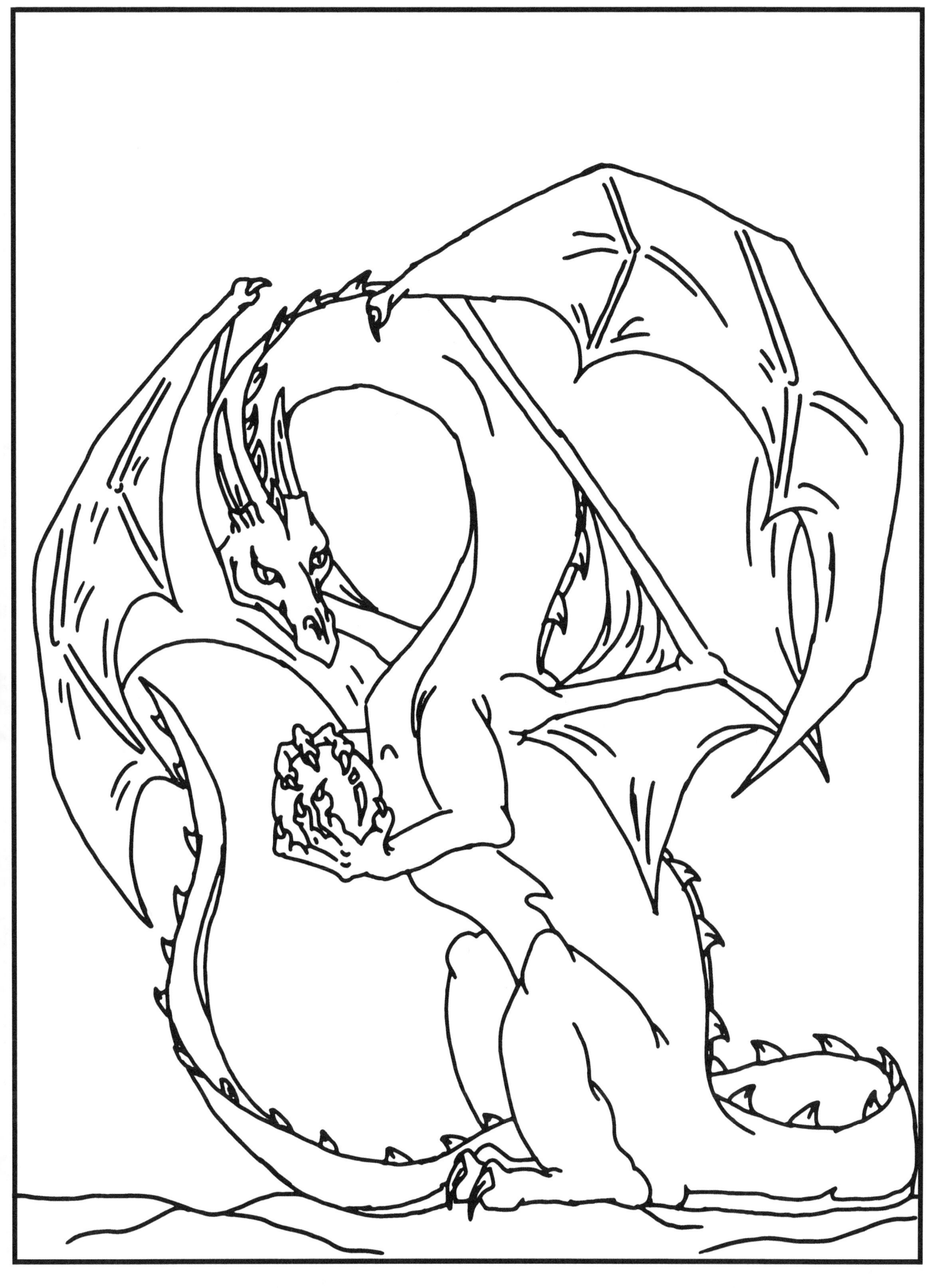

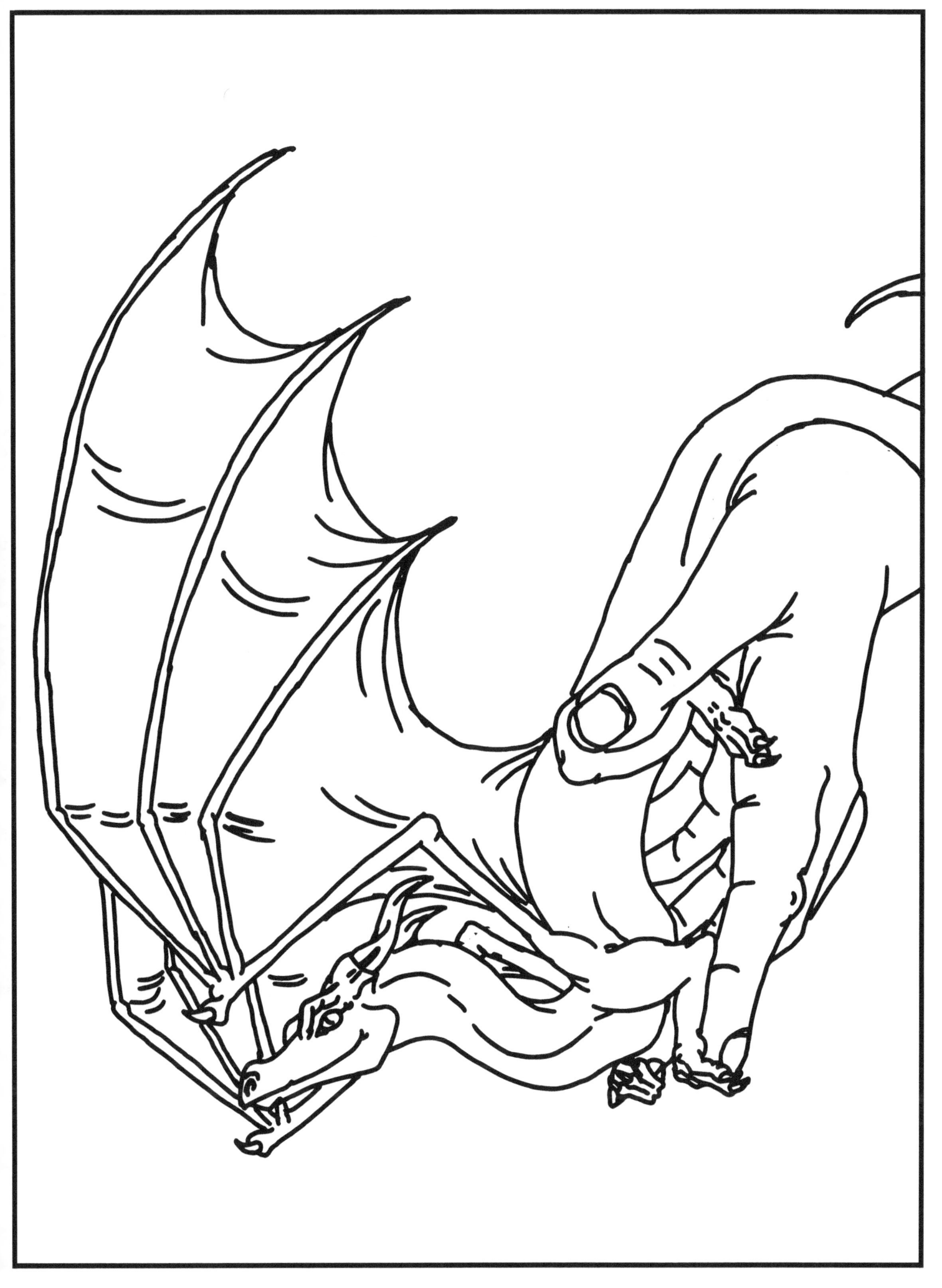

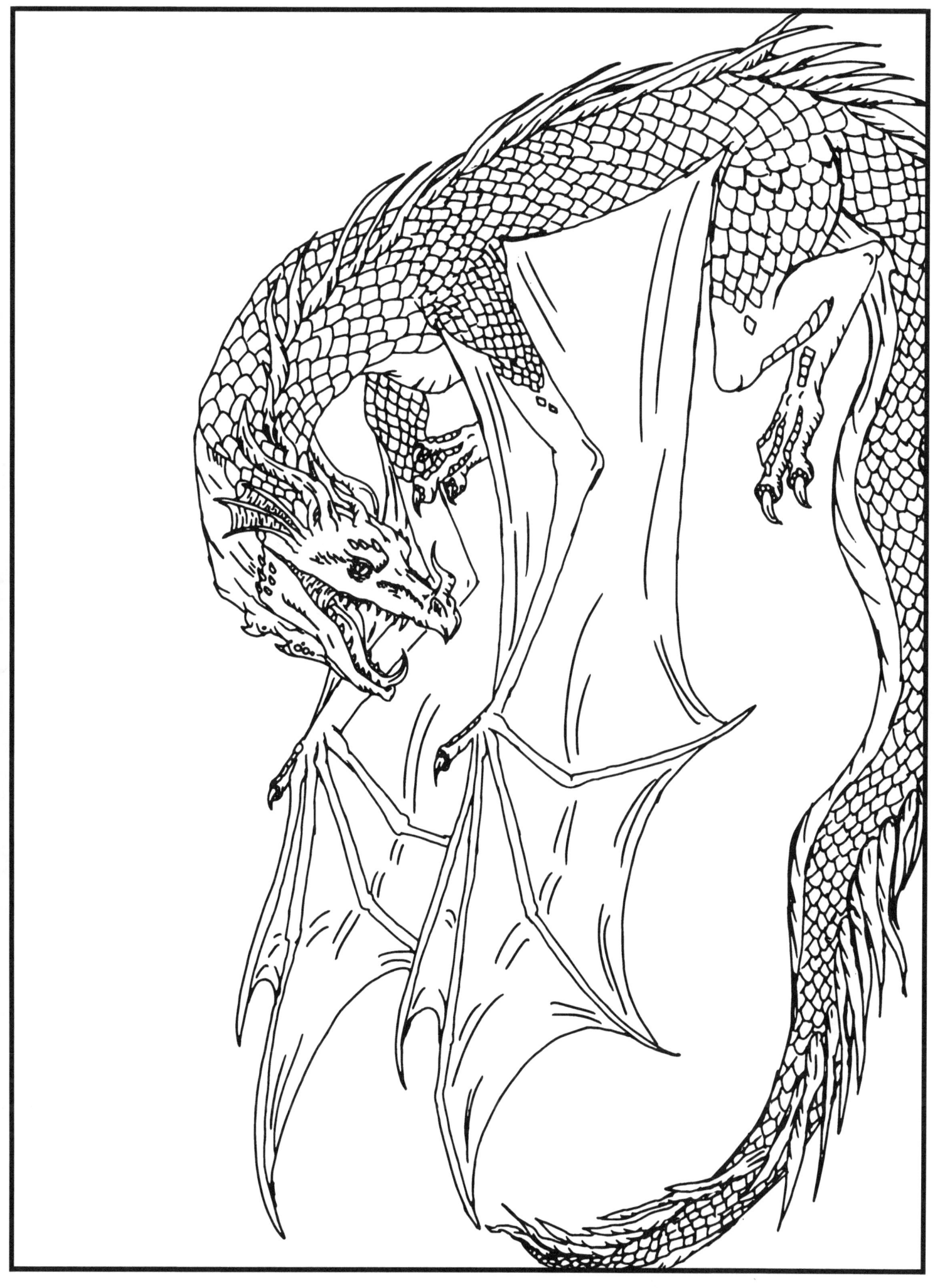

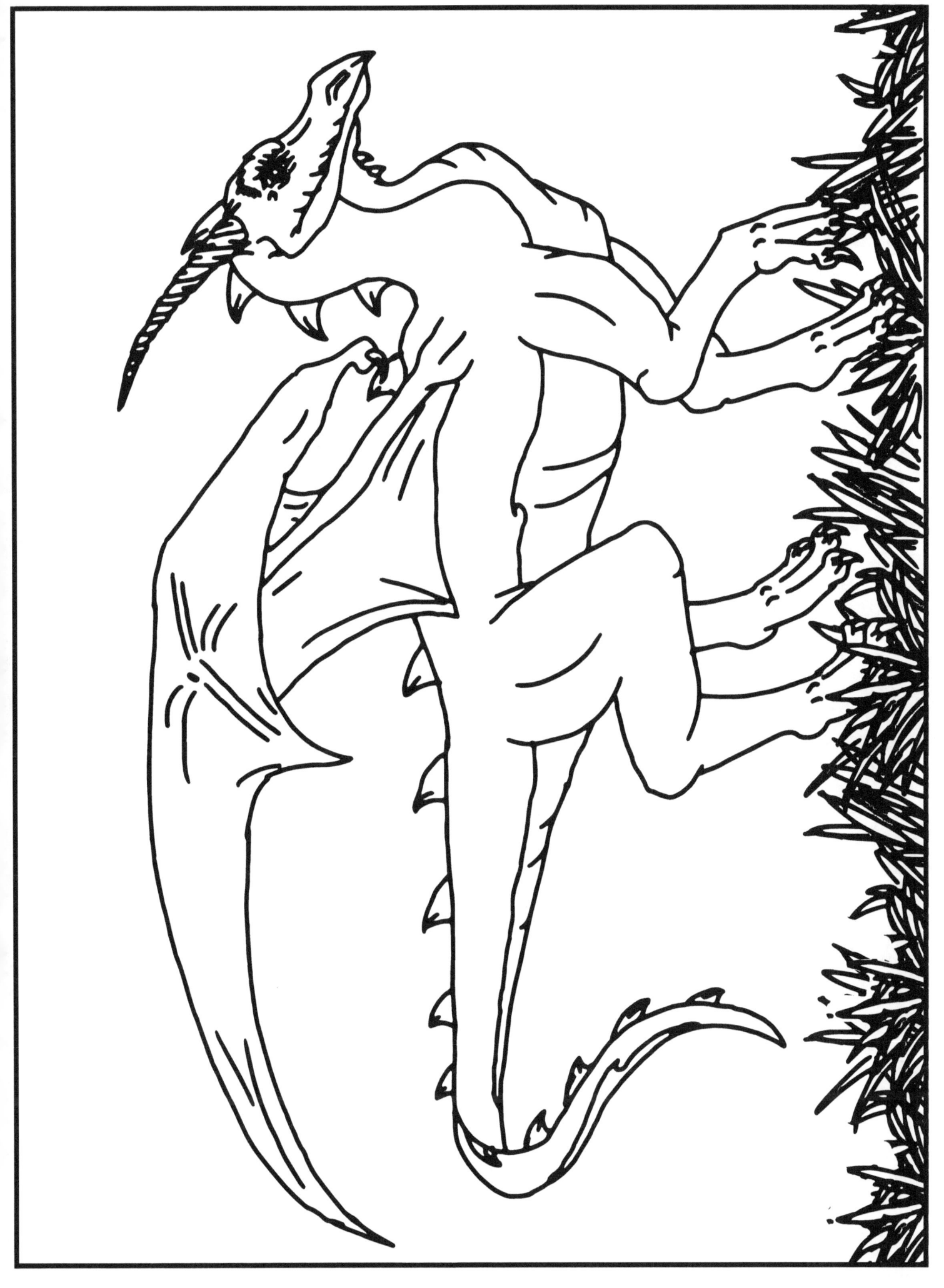

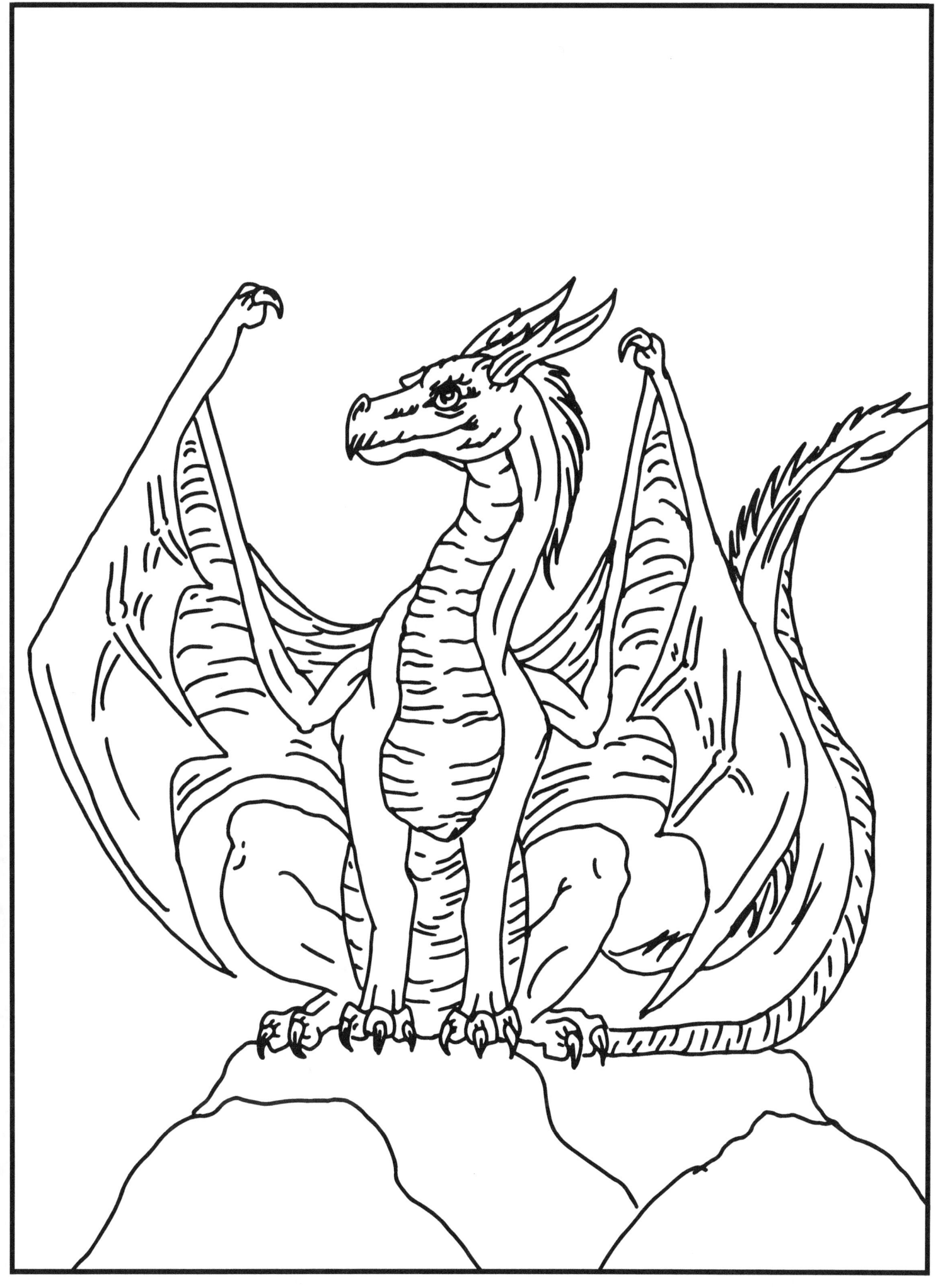

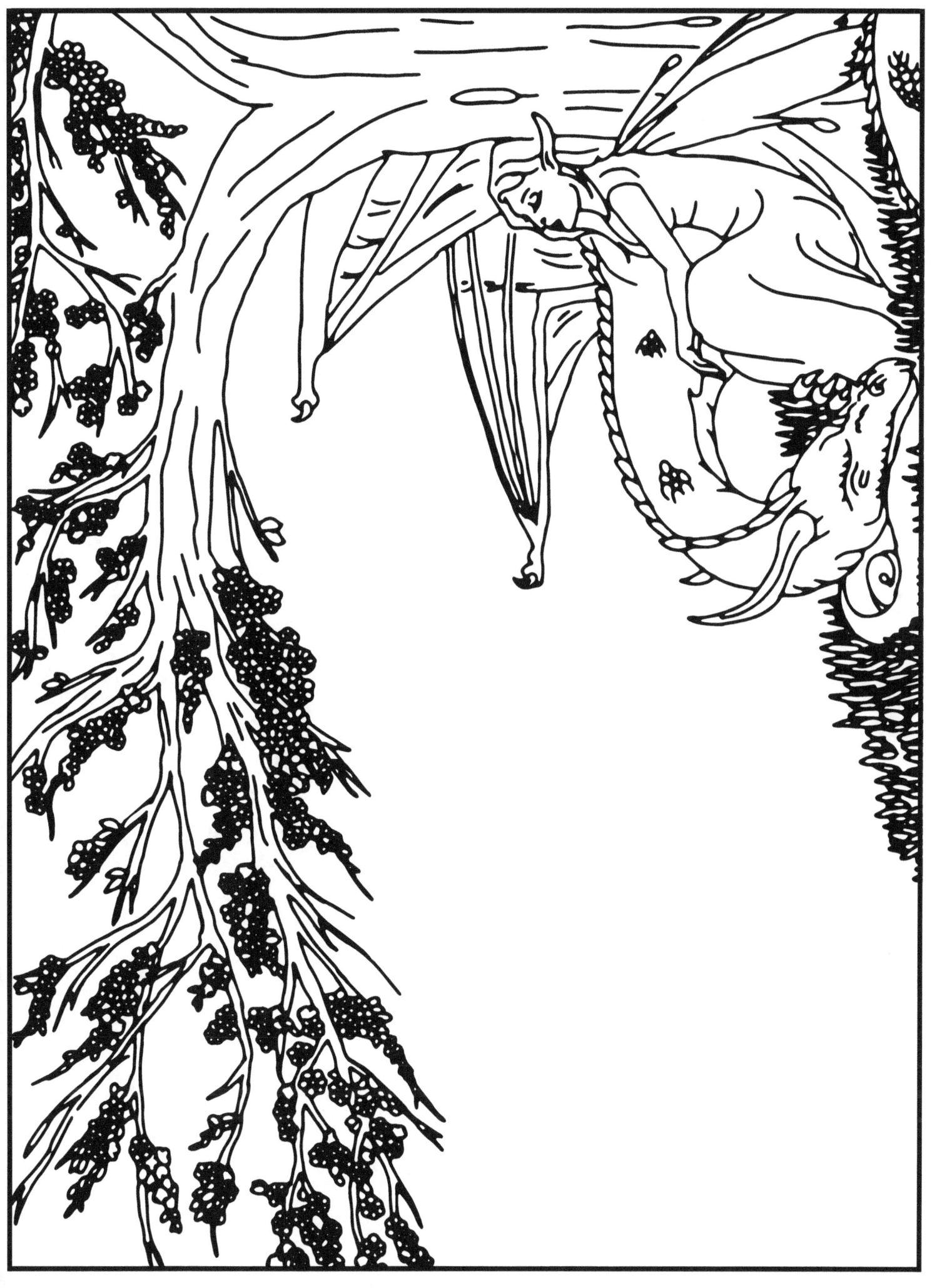

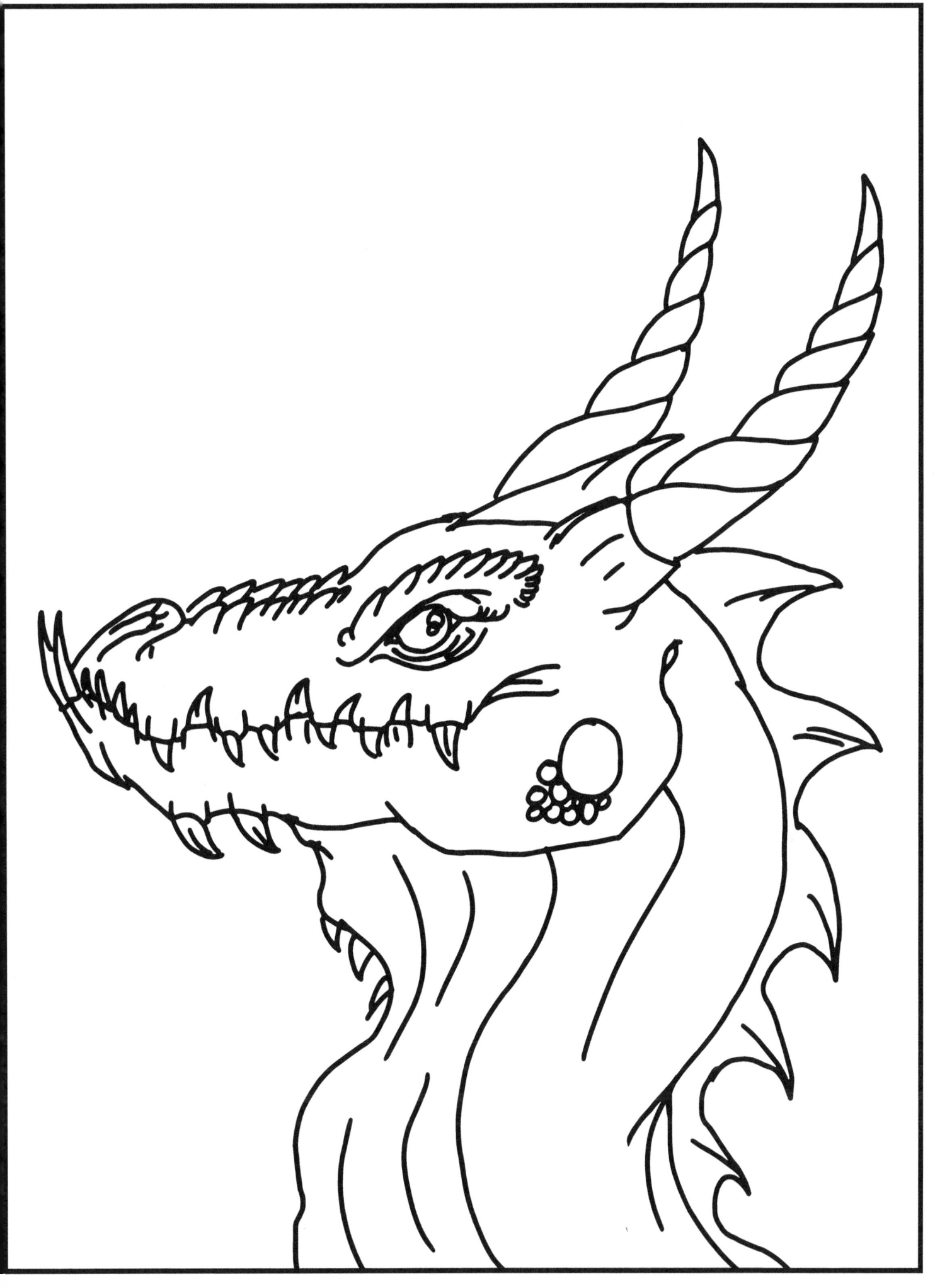

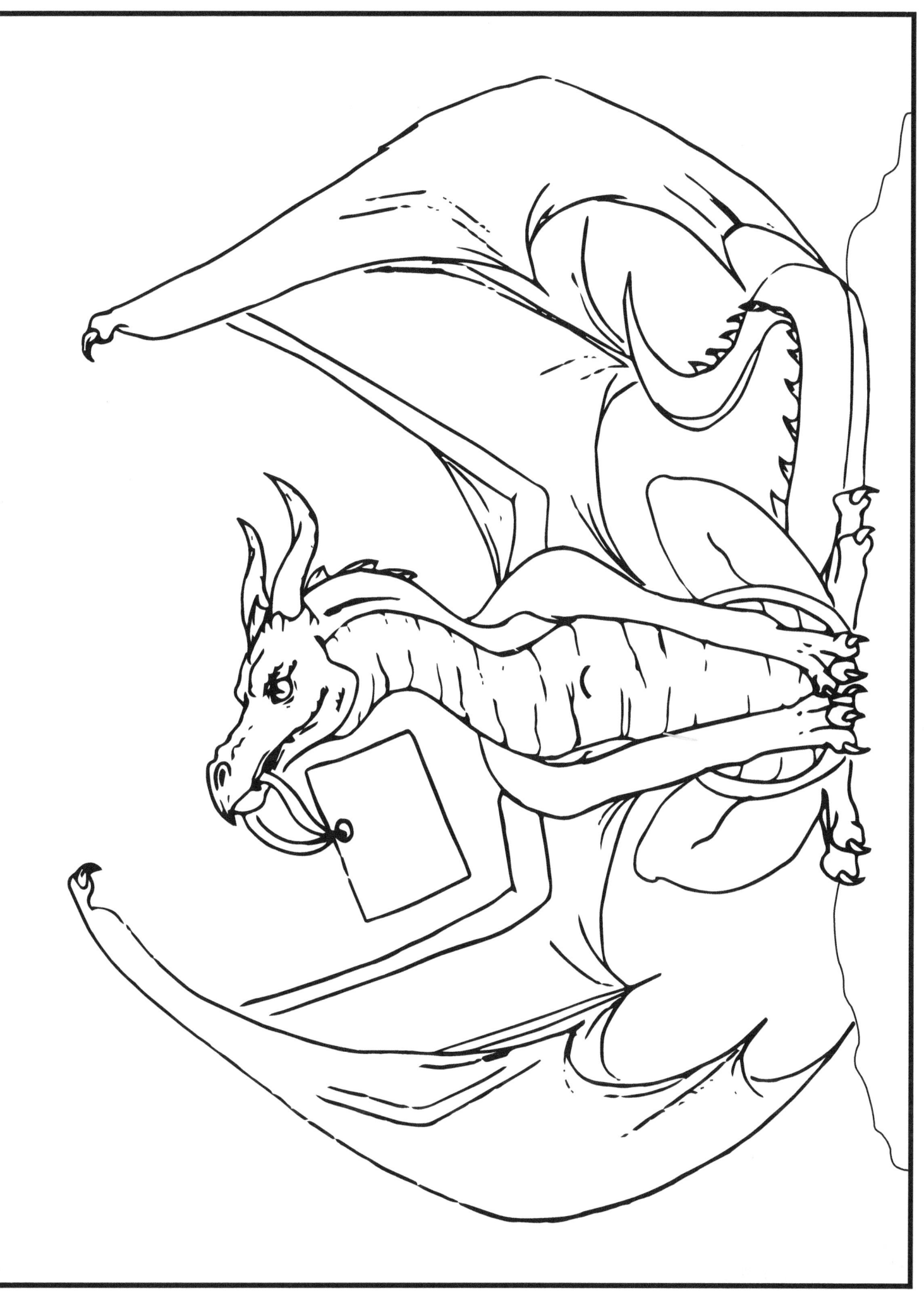